Mara

W9-BNN-575

GENERATION
REVOLUTION

GENERATION REVOLUTION

On the Front Line Between Tradition
and Change in the Middle East

Rachel Aspden

Other Press
New York

Library of Congress Cataloging-in-Publication Data

Names: Aspden, Rachel, author
Title: Generation revolution : on the front line between tradition and
change in the Middle East / Rachel Aspden.
Description: First American hardcover edition. | New York : Other Press,
2016. | Includes bibliographical references.
Identifiers: LCCN 2016024349 | ISBN 9781590518557 (hardcover)
| ISBN 9781590518564 (e-book)
Subjects: LCSH: Egypt—History—Protests, 2011- | Egypt—Social
conditions—21st century. | Revolutions—Egypt—History—21st century.
| Youth—Political activity—Egypt—History—21st century. | Youth—
Egypt—Social conditions—21st century.
Classification: LCC DT107.88 .A76 2016 | DDC 962.05/5—dc23 LC
record available at https://lccn.loc.gov/2016024349

For the people of Egypt who showed me so much kindness.
And for my grandparents.

CONTENTS

CONTENTS

PROLOGUE

I am proud of you as the new generation calling for a change for the better, dreaming and making the future.

Hosni Mubarak, president of Egypt, televised address to protesters, February 10, 2011

If the people one day wanted to live then destiny must respond and the night must fade away and the chains must break.

Tunisian poet Aboul Qassim Echebbi (1909–34), lines adopted as a chant in the Tunisian uprising of late 2010, then in protests in Egypt, Syria and Iraq

As the twenty-first century began, Egypt was ruled by old men. The president, Hosni Mubarak, was well into his seventies. Aging generals, bureaucrats and businessmen ran everything from the army to universities, tourist resorts and oil and gas installations. Even the leader of the most popular opposition movement, the banned Muslim Brotherhood, was the same age as Mubarak. And each of these men in his sphere—from police officers to religious scholars to fathers— expected deference and unquestioning obedience.

But Egypt was young. Of the 70 million Egyptians—a population that dwarfed every other in the Middle East except those of Iran and Turkey—almost two-thirds were under thirty. They had no political voice, limited job prospects and less hope. A gap was opening up between them and the men who controlled their lives.

I first arrived in Egypt in the autumn of 2003. I was twenty-three, I had just graduated and, six months earlier, I had watched on the television news as coalition tanks rolled into Iraq. This struggle, British prime minister Tony Blair told us, was existential, our enemy the Islamic extremists who "detest our freedom, democracy and tolerance." The solution? Exporting, by force if necessary, what he called "the universal values of the human spirit."[1]

I wanted to discover some of the truth about the Middle East for myself, and Cairo, the sprawling ancient city at its heart, was my starting point. I had never been to Egypt before, I knew no one and I spoke no Arabic, but I was eager to learn and ready for adventure. So I enrolled in a scruffy Arabic school and found a low-paid job on an English-language news magazine with two bored secret policemen parked permanently outside the office, smoking cheap cigarettes and eating chicken shwarma sandwiches.

I had landed in a desert in the deep freeze. Mubarak, a former air-force officer, had been in power for twenty-two years. All power and money flowed through the army and those close to it. Beyond its circle of privilege, half the population scraped an existence below or on the poverty line, and all but the wealthiest struggled with soaring food prices, unemployment, corruption and crumbling public services.

This status quo was cemented by around $1.5 billion of American aid a year,[2] the political support of the West and the rich Gulf monarchies, and the sprawling military, police and intelligence apparatus this patronage had helped create. It was hard to see how it could ever change. Political participation was tightly controlled, and dissenters risked abduction, torture, imprisonment or even death. It was a scene replicated across the Middle East. Though Saddam Hussein had just been removed by the United States, his fellow dictators—Muammar Gaddafi in Tripoli, Bashar al-Assad in Damascus, Zine al-Abidine Ben Ali in Tunis, Ali Abdullah Saleh in Sana'a and the monarchs in their gleaming Gulf cities—locked the region's balance of power in place.

But I could see that in other ways Egypt was on the point of change. Burger Kings, Costa Coffees and Starbucks were opening in middle-class districts, satellite TV channels were multiplying and more and more Egyptians had access to the Internet. It was getting harder for the regime to isolate them from new ideas and from each other, and to keep their desire for a share of the freedom and prosperity they saw on their screens in check.

The graduates of my own age who I met intrigued me.[3] In some ways our lives were alike—we used the same phones, watched the same Hollywood films, wore the same trainers and ate the same fast food—but they were struggling with very different pressures that flowed from the revival of conservative Islam and the deep-rooted traditions that still governed Egyptian society. They wanted to feel part of the twenty-first-century globalized world, but also—seeing the West invade their region and criticize their faith while propping up Egypt's corrupt and repressive government— to defend their identities as Muslims, Arabs and Egyptians. Religion and consumerism, tradition and modernity were pulling them in painfully different directions.

I began to think that their answers to these dilemmas would determine much about the region's future. If I wanted to understand more about the Middle East, I needed to listen to them.

I left Egypt in 2005 to work for a news magazine in London and spent the next six years traveling between the UK and the Middle East—through Syria, Lebanon, Jordan and Palestine, down to Sudan and across to the Gulf and Yemen. The stories of the young people I met reflected the same conflicts I had first heard about in Egypt, to where I found myself returning again and again. I started tracing the lives of a handful of young Egyptians—devout or atheist, apolitical or activist, conservative or liberal, but all middle-class city-dwelling students and graduates who were not isolated from outside influences like the rural poor or insulated from dysfunction like its country-hopping elite. In twenty or thirty years they would be leading their country, and I wanted to see where they would take it. The first half of this book follows them through the last years of Mubarak's Egypt, as they created the conditions for change.

Their chance to shape Egypt's future came sooner than anyone had expected. At the beginning of 2011, the uprisings that became known in the West as the Arab Spring made these young people, briefly, global heroes. The break with the old ways was fierce and certain. Caught up in their optimism, I moved back to Cairo to follow them full-time. Now the freeze had melted, what kind of state did they want to live in, what kind of lives did they want to lead, and what were they prepared to do to make it happen? The second half of this book tells their stories as they face the new Egypt of the revolution.

For the first time in their lives, they now had a political voice. But beyond the turmoil of parties, factions and elections that followed Mubarak's overthrow, I wanted to know about the personal beliefs and choices that would shape Egypt less directly but just as surely. I wanted to understand why a woman with three degrees might wear a face veil and conceal her hands with black gloves; why a start-up entrepreneur might demand his bride-to-be was a certified virgin; why a nightclub-going, hash-smoking student might despise the idea of democracy.

The weighing up went both ways. However hard I tried to fit in, I always stood out as non-Egyptian and non-Muslim. State propaganda about "foreign hands" meant some people assumed I was a UK government spy, others that I was serving a shadowy private agenda. I understood their reticence, because talking about the wrong subject—anything from military service to sex—could bring not only retribution from state security but censure and shame from friends and family. For this reason, some names and other identifying details in this book have been altered or omitted.

As violence escalated, the space the uprisings had opened up to imagine different ways of being and doing was rapidly closing. Though the Muslim Brotherhood had come to power by the ballot box, their increasing authoritarianism helped opponents at home and in the West invoke the shadow of the Iranian revolution—a broad-based opposition movement that had toppled over into purges, executions and the creation of a theocratic state.

After the summer of 2013, when the army seized power once more and one thousand protesters were killed in central Cairo by the security forces, Egypt was gripped by cruelty and fear. Journalists and activists were arrested or disappeared. Some of the people I was following emigrated, some lay low, others became fervent supporters of the new military president, Abdel Fattah el-Sisi. They saw the bloody chaos in Syria, Iraq and Libya, and the bombings and shootings in Egypt itself, and believed that only a return to the old ways could save them. Another freeze was settling, grimmer than the one I'd experienced in 2003.

By the time I left in 2015, the world didn't believe that young Egyptians—or Tunisians or Yemenis or particularly Syrians—were heroes anymore. Now young European Muslims, including teenage girls from the school facing my old apartment in London, were traveling to join Islamic State in Syria and Iraq. In the opposite direction, tens of thousands of Middle Eastern refugees were fleeing to Europe. Young men trained in the war that displaced them wrought carnage in Paris and threatened the rest of Europe. The stakes were higher than ever. Where war and upheaval in the Middle East had once seemed comfortably distant, Western countries were now being forced to ask their own questions about the relationship between Islam and democracy, global culture and local tradition, what "rights" and "freedom" mean, and what the ideal society could and should look like. The stories in this book take place in Egypt, but they have—unexpectedly—become about the West as well.

PART ONE

1

Amal and Nayera:
Women in a Man's World

"Who in this room doesn't pray five times a day?" the teacher demanded. His eyes raked the classroom. "Stand up now."

The teenagers shuffled nervously in their seats and looked at the floor or their hands. They were all Muslim, but many of them failed to complete each prayer before the next call to prayer, as scholars had determined they must in the earliest days of Islam. They knew far better than to admit this. But Amal was tired of being forced to lie. She stood up.

"I don't always pray all the prayers," she said. "Why are you asking?"

The teacher stared at her. Her boldness was shocking, but he saw only a small sixteen-year-old girl, her freckled face framed by a headscarf.

"This is a disgrace," he shouted. "You know it is your duty as a Muslim to pray." He called her forward and beat her with a ruler in front of the other students.

Later that day, another teacher visited them. His eyes also raked the room, passing over the boys who made up four-fifths of the class. Egyptian schools are usually single-sex, but in small villages there is often not enough money or space for segregation.

"You should all be dressing modestly, according to the laws of Islam," he said quietly, staring at the girls. "And what that means is a *khimar*. Anything less—you may think

9

you're dressed, but you're almost naked." The *khimar* is a big, shapeless cloak that drapes over a woman's head and falls over her arms to below her waist. It is always a drab, muddy color—navy, dirty olive, sludge brown. Amal hated those colors almost as much as the stifling folds of the cloak itself. Like a few of the other girls, she covered her head with a scarf alone. When the teacher left the room, the boys started to bang on the desks. The relief of escaping punishment and humiliation made them quick to gloat over those who had been less fortunate.

"They're dressed, they're dressed but they're almost naked!" they shouted, pointing at the girls who weren't wearing a *khimar*.

It was the end of the 1990s and Amal lived with her family in a village in the Fayoum oasis sixty miles (100 kilometers) south of Cairo. As she walked home through its garbage-strewn mud streets with her brother and younger sisters, Amal felt afraid. Now, the boys were hitting the desks. The next time, she thought, they might be hitting her. She looked at the walls of the cement-block houses they passed, decorated with childlike folk paintings of minarets, misshapen airplanes and ferry boats and the black cube of the Kaaba shrine, showing that the inhabitant had made the hajj pilgrimage to Mecca. The *khimar* the teacher wanted her to wear was no traditional garment but a 1970s invention designed to demonstrate the wearer's piety as well as liberating her from the expense and distraction of following secular fashion.[1] Now many people were beginning to believe that, like the hajj, it had always been required by God.

Ever since the oil boom of the 1970s, Egyptians of all social classes, including taxi drivers, construction workers and domestic servants from Amal's village, had been traveling as migrant laborers to the Gulf. When they returned home, many brought its more austere, rigid customs and belief system with them. And now, well-funded preachers spreading Salafism, Saudi Arabia's fundamentalist interpretation of Islam, were beginning to appear in Egyptian mosques and on the popular cassettes of sermons sold from street stalls. But this new religious orthodoxy dovetailed with deeper-rooted convictions. The Coptic Christian minority who made up around 10% of Egyptians[2] were hardly less conservative than their neighbours, and, especially in the villages of what Egyptians called the Sa'id—the sweltering 600-mile (1,000-kilometer) stretch of southern Egypt that began with the Fayoum—they also participated in the unknown number of honor killings that went largely unreported to the police and unpunished by the courts.

Amal didn't want to wear a *khimar* but she had no desire to be beaten or insulted by her teachers, her classmates or anyone else.

"Dad, I really need to wear the *khimar*," she told her father as soon as she got home. Her father was kind, and he had far less rigid beliefs about religion than her teachers. But he believed as strongly as everyone else in the clear hierarchy of authority that governed society from top to bottom. Just as faithful Muslims submitted to God, the people to the president, farmers and workers to the elite, women to men, his authority in the family was never questioned.

"No," he said. "You wear a headscarf, and that's quite enough. There's no reason for anything more." The way things were already done, in his eyes, was the way they should stay.

"But Dad," Amal began. Her stomach flipped over at the thought of facing the teachers and boys without a *khimar*.

"I said no," he repeated firmly.

Amal had to save her pocket money, hoarding the few dollars her father gave her each week until she had enough to buy the big, ugly cloak. She hid it from her parents, and put it on when she went to school in the mornings. She was learning that the punishment for honesty was harsh, and that the best way around inflexible rules was outward compliance and surreptitious disobedience. To survive, she would have to sacrifice her own desires and beliefs to fulfill the expectations of the society around her. But unlike many of her friends she still, secretly, kept her desire for freedom.

While Amal donned her *khimar*, the state's vision of a modern Egyptian woman was quite different. It had been shaped along with the military regime itself under Gamal Abdel Nasser in the 1950s and '60s, when Paris and Rome had set the trends in the chic districts of Cairo and Alexandria. Now, in the late 1990s, female employees of state TV and the national airline EgyptAir were still banned from wearing even a headscarf, let alone a *khimar* or face veil. In elite circles overtly Islamic dress was considered frumpy and déclassé, a mark of bigotry and, worse, insularity.

The official face of women's rights was the bareheaded, glamorously made-up, half-Welsh First Lady Suzanne Mubarak. Her choice of causes—at least in the eyes of the West and the Egyptian elite—was beyond reproach. She campaigned against female genital mutilation,[3] which was still legal and had been performed on around nine out of ten adult Egyptian women;[4] for improving literacy, as less than half of Egyptian women were literate, against two-thirds of men; and for legislation giving women more equal divorce and custody rights and introducing a parliamentary quota for women. The international community applauded, and showered her with awards.

But at home, her initiatives were the mark of a state that was losing touch with its citizens. Suzanne Mubarak was completely out of step with the realities of life for ordinary Egyptian women.[5] Not only did the glossy campaigns make no mention of the cruelty and corruption of her husband's regime, the kind of liberated lifestyle she promoted was unimaginable in a down-at-heel provincial village like Amal's—or even in the overcrowded working-class districts a few miles from the presidential palace in Cairo. In many Egyptians' minds, secularism was becoming increasingly inseparable from repression. After three decades of growing conservatism, "women's rights" and "feminism" were easily dismissed as alien and hostile inventions of the West— especially when they were promoted by someone who looked like the First Lady. Hard-line Islamic teachings reinforced the traditional belief that men and women had different "natures," responsibilities and, consequently, degrees of freedom. "Women's rights" were an assault on this natural order ordained by God and approved by man.

Perversely, the rise of conservative Islam in Egypt had been hastened by the regime itself. Though the military state was nominally Muslim, it had wrestled with political Islam and its violent offshoots ever since the army officer Gamal Abdel Nasser had taken power after his 1952 coup against the British-backed monarchy. Mubarak was a front-row witness to this struggle, having been seated next to his predecessor Anwar Sadat when the president was gunned down by a jihadi cell in October 1981. He promised Egyptians security and stability, but they soon found he had no grand political project to inspire their devotion, and few promises of prosperity to buy it. Real wealth was skimmed off by the military and the corrupt elite, while tens of millions of poor bore the brunt of corruption and repression. In the vacuum, conservative Islam began to flourish, promising justice, righteousness and community as well as the more tangible benefits, such as subsidized health care and food supplies, distributed by many Islamic organizations.

Not all of them were peaceful. During the 1990s the Fayoum, where Amal lived, and the cities along the Nile Valley to its south, harbored radical jihadi groups that attacked soldiers, police, civilians and, increasingly, the foreign tourists on whom the Egyptian economy relied. In 1997 sixty-two people, most of them tourists, were shot and hacked to death in a temple in Luxor. This was how the state portrayed Islamists—as barbarian fanatics who emerged from their desert hideouts to wreak destruction on civilized people. But at the same time, the Muslim Brotherhood—banned, but operating semi-legally—was working to create a moderate Islamist political opposition and expand its charitable and preaching networks throughout Egypt.

All these currents were combining to create the gradual sea change in beliefs and behavior that led to Amal's state-school teacher ordering her to wear the *khimar*. And Mubarak's regime tolerated these changes—which, for the moment, were concentrated among the poor—as a convenient distraction from their discontents. Maintaining stability required a delicate balancing act—as long as they steered clear of violence or politics, citizens were permitted a certain amount of leeway before they were brought to heel.

In 2003, I arrived in Cairo in the midst of this slow groundswell of conservatism. I had landed in a city far more chaotic and a society far more controlled than those I was used to. Like every Western visitor for centuries, I was stunned by the heat, the crowds, the dust and the uproar of outdoor life in the streets, teahouses and markets. As I slowly oriented myself, I realized that in this metropolis of 15 million people, the idea of "privacy" barely existed, while social bonds and social judgments were everything. On packed metro carriages or battered microbuses strangers slumped on each other's shoulders or demanded a drink from each other's water bottles; neighbors avidly spied on and gossiped about each other; and *bawab*s, the omnipresent doorman-porter-guards who sat at every apartment building's door, monitored residents' every move.

As a Westerner I had a level of privilege and protection that flowed from what Egyptians, remembering their French and British colonizers, called the "foreigner complex." But as soon as I stepped out of my front door I also had an unwelcome share in the experience of being a woman in Egypt. Because I happened to be female, I was now surrounded by people who wanted to dictate what I could do, say and wear; where I could go, who I could go with and when I could go there; where I could sit in public; how I could travel; what time I could enter and leave my house and who I could invite there— and the finely gauged range of disapproval, harassment and intimidation they could mete out if I crossed these boundaries.

Most of these strictures had little to do with formal Islamic teaching. But growing conservatism encouraged judgment of all women not seen to embody the feminine virtues of obedience and *haya'*, modesty. Living away from my family—as was normal for young people in the West, but not in Egypt—I found that many men assumed that a woman with no male "protection" was an easy source of sex for those with the initiative to take it. When I rented an apartment with two other European women, neighbors tore pornographic pictures out of magazines and threw them onto our balcony, along with empty Viagra packets. One morning I opened my shutters to find two men perched in the uppermost branches of the tree outside, comfortably positioned for the best view into my room. I had no idea how long they'd been there.

It was the state that had laid the ground for these sex-crazed citizens—like their puritanical mirror images—to run wild. While Suzanne Mubarak's projects made excellent international PR, the military men who made up the regime were far from serious about dismantling the patriarchal systems that reinforced their own power. Women were treated as second-class citizens by the police, the courts and the law itself. Sexual harassment and assault were not criminalized, the police dismissed reports of domestic violence and rape—and were themselves responsible for beating, sexually humiliating and raping detained men and women—men who killed adulterous wives could be released without punishment, and divorce laws ensured women could be left penniless and in some cases without a home or their children in the time it took a husband to say the phrase "I divorce you."

I wondered for a long time whether it was possible for a woman to openly defy the risks and censure, until I met Amal. She lived in a way that was unheard of for a woman not from a rich Westernized background. She owned her own flat, where she lived alone, and rented a spare room out to foreign flatmates. She drove a car that she'd bought herself, taught English in an expensive private school and no longer wore a headscarf.

I thought Amal was brave and admirable, because her choices and achievements appealed to every individualistic Western instinct I had. But some female friends in Cairo rolled their eyes when I mentioned her—"Why would I want to live apart from my parents, when I love them? Or pay for everything myself? What do you think is so great about that?" they asked—and others winced sympathetically. "Unfortunately, no man will ever agree to marry her," they said. They knew it was close to impossible for any Egyptian to exist outside a protective network of family, friends and neighbors. Isolation was suspicious, and people had little sympathy for tearaways, outcasts and pioneers. Amal's story showed the forces that kept them in their place.

Growing up in the village, Amal had seen her entire future mapped out ahead of her. Unlike some of her friends, she would be allowed to go to university, but the end result would be the same. After graduating, she would marry a local man approved by her parents, from a respectable family, with a steady job and enough money to pay a dower and buy and furnish a simple flat in the village. Then she would cook and care for her husband and the children she would bear as soon as possible. Her education would not go to waste—it would increase her value in the marriage market.

All Amal's school friends knew what would happen to them in a few years' time, and they clustered together at breaktime to speculate about the men who would determine the course of their future lives. Some girls were cheerfully resigned.

"Some men are relaxed—they let you be boss at home, even if they're boss outside the house," said one optimistically. "OK, you can't go out without his permission, but inside the house you can manage everything just the way you like."

The girls who were badly beaten by their fathers and brothers had more modest ambitions—they dreamed only of marrying a man who wouldn't hit them or curse them as their families did.

"As long as he doesn't do these things, he can be boss inside and outside the house, I don't care," said a skinny girl who sometimes came to school with bruises turning purple and yellow on her cheekbones.

Other girls had romantic dreams about a life of bliss with a handsome, sensitive soulmate. Pragmatic Amal thought this was stupid. She had seen how marriages ended up in the Fayoum.

"Look at all of our parents, at our aunts and uncles and their husbands and wives. Do they seem so happy to you? You think that you will somehow magically not end up just like them?" she asked.

"Why are you so bitter, Amal? My marriage won't be like that. We'll be in love."

Amal couldn't stop herself. "Even if you meet someone and fall in love, your family won't let you marry him. They'll bring someone they think is more suitable, and they'll pressure you and pressure you to marry him. And eventually you'll give in. You won't be different, you will be just the same as everyone else."

The girls just looked at her like she was crazy.

None of the girls Amal knew had ever thought of rebelling against their families' faith in the way things were done. The prospect of a ruined reputation, social rejection and no hope of a "good" marriage was too terrifying. Their parents weren't cruel, and they wanted their daughters to be happy in the only way they could imagine. But the world was changing, and their expectations hadn't caught up with it. Slowly, satellite TV and the Internet were reaching even backwaters like the village, bringing pictures of unimaginably different lives. Amal thought that if she could just get out of the Fayoum, she might have a chance to choose her own future. English, she thought, might be the key to her escape: a chance to connect with the outside world, and maybe even to find a well-paid modern job. When she was seventeen, she was admitted to study English at Cairo University.

Everyone in Amal's village looked and sounded the same and believed in the same things. But at university she saw that traditions varied across Egypt, which made them feel even more arbitrary and unfair. Now she took classes with Muslim girls from Alexandria and Suez who had never worn the veil because their fathers didn't believe it was an Islamic obligation. Amal had gratefully taken off the *khimar* when she left school, and she wondered what it would be like to wear no scarf at all. One day at university she took it off, braving the stares of the other students from her village, who had never seen her without it.

"*Rabenna yehdiki!*" they told her, shocked. "May God guide you!"

Worse awaited her at home, where the family's honor rested on the reputation of Amal and her sisters. When Amal tried to leave the house for university bareheaded, her brother and her parents barred her way.

"You can't go out like that," her mother told her, holding her arm imploringly. "What will people say about us? Please see sense and put your scarf on."

"I won't," said Amal. "This is what I want to wear. A lot of the other girls dress like this."

"It's simple then," replied her father. His tone was flat and final. "You won't go anywhere." Just like he hadn't wanted her to wear the *khimar*, he didn't want her to take off the headscarf, because that was what respectable women from their village wore. Amal sat in her room, humiliated and angry. *I feel like someone has tied my hands and feet together*, she thought to herself. But her family was her only source of shelter, food, support and safety. So she swallowed her fury and decided to compromise again. The next day she went out the door unhindered, dressed as they wanted in her headscarf.

On her long microbus journeys to and from university, squashed uncomfortably against the window with her bag of textbooks wedged on top of her, Amal thought more and more about the unfeminine subject of money. It would not change the beliefs of those around her, but having her own money would give her greater status and significance within her family—and perhaps she could use it to buy herself some freedom. Finding work was not easy. Half of young women were unemployed, and many graduates waited months or years before finding a job. Her father had no wealthy friends he could ask to employ her in their businesses; no influential connections he could leverage for a bureaucratic job in a government office.

For the moment, Amal decided, any job would do. When she graduated in 2003, she felt lucky to find work teaching English in the state primary school in her village, even though the salary was so tiny it barely paid for her stationery supplies. But from the start, it was a disaster. The kind of beatings that Amal had suffered at school were considered the mark of a competent teacher, and parents and the other staff were outraged by her refusal to dole them out.

"You're ruining their morals! If you treat them in this soft way they'll never learn anything!" shouted her supervisor. "You must hit them, scream at them." Amal remembered the teacher who had beaten her for not praying all the prayers, and she felt disgusted not just with her village but with all of Egypt. *I have to get out of this country*, she thought. *I can never make any money here, I have no freedom and people treat each other in a terrible way. There's nothing here for me but unhappiness.* Confiding in her family or friends was pointless; to escape Egypt, she needed the help of foreigners. Secretly, she contacted the handful she knew for advice. A young Canadian woman Amal had met at a university event turned out to be a member of an international church in Cairo. With the congregation's help, Amal quickly found a job teaching English in the last place she could ever have imagined—a language school in Beijing.

Step by step, the plan unfolded. Her new friends from the church lent her money for the ticket. She told her parents she had been offered a job teaching in Dubai, and pleaded for permission to take it. Though it was shameful for them to allow their daughter to travel alone, her parents knew that the rewards could be considerable. The Emirates is a Muslim country, which would mute criticism from the extended family and neighbors. And, after all, the family needed money. Her parents agreed she could work in Dubai for one year, and Amal set off for China. It was the first time she had left Egypt, the first time she had flown on a plane.

From the moment she set foot in Beijing, she was elated by her newfound freedom. She loved the incomprehensible flow of Mandarin around her, the neon signs and the metro and the crowded streets. She loved her Chinese students, who studied hard and uncomplainingly. She loved having her own money to spend however she wanted. And she loved being finally liberated from the constant exhausting scrutiny of what she wore, said and did. She wore T-shirts and shorts instead of long robes and headscarves, rode a bike to work without ruining her marriage prospects, went to restaurants and parties and karaoke bars with other young teachers without anyone cursing her as a prostitute. She bought snacks from street carts which looked just like those in the Fayoum, but instead of fava beans or falafel, they sold delicious greasy meat sandwiched in steamed buns.

"Amal, did you know that that's pork?" a colleague asked her. She spat out the bun, horrified. Pork was unclean, a diseased, filthy meat that no good Muslim would dream of touching. Then she thought about it. Her upbringing told her pork was dirty, but it tasted so good. Her upbringing had been wrong about so many things. Happily, she went back to the steamed buns.

But the happiness didn't last. The school began paying the teachers late, or not enough, or not at all. Some, far from home, were too afraid to complain, but Amal was stubborn and she refused to work until she was properly paid. Her friends panicked, warning her that if she made trouble the school would simply summon the police and have her deported. Seeking a way out, Amal called her parents, who still thought she was in Dubai, making money for the family.

"Everything's terrible here," she told them down the crackly phone line to the village. "I'm so unhappy. I really want to come home."

"No," said her father. "You went for a year, you have to see it through."

"But I can't, things are so bad," said Amal. She started to cry.

"Stay for the rest of the year, then you can come back," he said. "That's final."

A week later Amal was deported at her own expense. She landed back in Cairo with no money and nowhere to go.

Her friends from the church rescued her again, finding her a job as a live-in nanny with a rich Egyptian family. She would save some money, Amal planned, and contact her parents when her agreed time in "Dubai" was up. Then the state stepped in. For years, tension between Egypt's Muslims and the Christian minority had found an outlet in manufactured moral panics. In the lurid tales of the tabloids, pure Muslim girls were constantly at risk of being seduced away from their faith by lecherous Christian men. The paranoia could easily escalate to riots, lynchings and church burnings. Unknown to Amal, state security officers were monitoring the church, looking for Muslim girls who had gone astray. As she came out of a service with her friends one day, they swooped.

"It has nothing to do with changing religion," Amal protested when the officers seized her. "It's just having fun and meeting people." It was no use. As for everyone else in Egypt, her birth religion was clearly recorded on her state identity card. Though Amal was over twenty-one and legally an adult, they took her to a police station and called her father, as the male responsible for her. Twelve hours later, she found herself once again in the Fayoum, her plans in ruins.

Back in the village, Amal's family were determined she would not escape and disgrace them again. They locked all the doors to the house, covered the windows with metal frames, and barred her bedroom door with pieces of heavy wood. Amal, in despair, refused to eat or drink. For days, she sat in her room, silent and growing weaker. Her parents panicked. They were traditional, but they were not like some of their neighbors, who would severely beat or even kill a daughter for disobedience that brought such shame upon the family. They just wanted Amal to be reasonable, not to die. They brought a girl from the village, an old school friend of Amal's, to reason with her.

"Just say you'll do what they want," she pleaded, frightened by how pale and sad Amal looked. "Then everything will be fine again."

Amal's father was listening in. He was worried about his daughter too.

"We're going to have an agreement," he told her. "We'll take away the locks and you can go to the village as long as someone else goes with you. You can even look for another job there. But you'll stay living here with us. No more running away, no more scandals."

Amal agreed meekly, because in the long hours in her room she had decided the only way to escape was to feign submission. The next day, she asked if she could go to the village to buy some things for her sisters. Then came the question her parents had been waiting to ask.

"If you want to buy things, where is the money you got from Dubai?" asked her mother.

Amal didn't have any. Her wages from China had gone on her deportation. She had saved a few hundred dollars from her nannying job. But this was her only hope, she thought, her stepping stone to freedom. There was no way she could hand it over to her family.

"I don't have any money," she told her parents. "The school stole it."

Her parents were distraught, but there was nothing they could do. All the upheaval and shame had been for nothing.

For the next weeks Amal watched and waited, outwardly docile. First, she was allowed to leave the house escorted by her mother. Then, by her younger sister. Eventually, she was allowed to run family errands to the nearby grocery by herself. Her parents saw her going and dutifully returning laden with bags and thought she had changed, that she would find a job in the village and that the family crisis was over. But, barely understanding all the uses of the Internet, they hadn't blocked the dial-up connection, and all the while Amal was secretly searching for jobs on the family's ancient PC. Soon, she had another position in China and a flight booked with the last of her savings. She told her parents she was going to the grocery, carrying only a handbag to avoid arousing their suspicions. Instead of returning with the week's supply of tea and cooking oil, she caught a bus to Cairo. When she got to the airport, she called them.

"I'm leaving," she told her father. "I'm at the airport, about to get on a plane to China."

The shouting started, and the orders to return. Then the tears and pleading.

"No," Amal said calmly. "I'm leaving now. Good-bye."

It was the hardest thing she had ever done, but she felt she had no choice. Compromise hadn't worked, she was exhausted by deception, and she was determined never again to end up nailed into her bedroom in the village, or being handed over to her father by state security. To live the life she dreamed of, she would have to seize it now, on her own terms.

The bonds of obedience were so strong that it took a radical act to break them.

By the time I met Amal in Cairo, several years after her escape to China, her defiance had at least partly paid off. She had worked in Beijing, then found a job teaching in Dubai—for real, this time—and worked weekends and overtime until she had saved up enough to buy a modest apartment in Cairo and a small car. She had sent enough money to her family for them to at first reluctantly accept her strange way of living, then ask eagerly if she could find jobs in Dubai for her sisters and brother too. Through sheer strength of will—allied with the access to the Internet, foreign contacts and the booming international English-tuition market that were newly available to her generation—she had transformed her life from the prospect of marriage and servitude in the village that had stretched ahead of her at sixteen. She still faced the same gossip and censure from neighbors and hate-filled harassment on the streets as every other woman in Cairo, but Amal was proud and satisfied. Her ability to make money was her key to freedom.

Few young women wanted to follow in her footsteps, and of those few, even fewer had the ruthless courage and determination to do so. The price of freedom of choice and of speech was high—and those who aspired to greater independence preferred to dream of an express route. Most of Amal's new middle-class friends in Cairo, they confessed to her, were looking for a nontraditional liberal man with the traditional attributes of wealth, good looks and social status who, after a nontraditional romantic courtship with his beloved, would observe the traditional pattern of meetings with her parents, buy the lavish jewelry traditionally presented to the bride, pay for the wedding and the new house the couple would inhabit, then whisk her away to a blissful future of liberation from her family. Amal rolled her eyes at them as she had at the romantic girls in her village, because it was a dream that was equally unlikely to come true.

At the same time, pressure to appear at least outwardly demure and conservative was increasing. As the 2000s wore on, more Egyptian girls and women began wearing the headscarf. This time it wasn't the poor or people in the villages, but middle-class and even wealthy upper-class women in the fashionable districts of Egypt's big cities. The spread of the headscarf, assumed to be a barometer for support for Islamist political movements, provoked anxiety across the Middle East's more secularly minded dictatorships. The Tunisian regime had outlawed polygamy, granted equal rights to divorce and legalized abortion—alongside banning the headscarf from schools and government buildings. In 2006, the president Zine al-Abidine Ben Ali launched a campaign to discourage women from wearing headscarves at all, and police stopped women in the street to tell them to bare their heads. Such tactics did as little to inspire love for the regime as Suzanne Mubarak's more measured efforts in Egypt. By 2007, an estimated nine out of ten Egyptian women were veiled.[6]

When I compared Amal to other young women I met in Cairo, raised in the city with wealthier, more liberal parents and wider opportunities, I understood how exceptional her story was. The well-heeled areas of the capital might seem far more freewheeling than rural backwaters like Amal's village, but I discovered how conservative they still were—especially when it came to the subjects of sex and marriage—when I met a loose group of friends that included a young woman, Nayera, and a young man, Abdel Rahman.

What I want to know is, why did Allah create girls with hymens? typed Nayera surreptitiously. It was past midnight, the only time she was ever alone, when her parents were finally asleep and her seventeen-year-old sister dozed in the bed beside hers. They had no idea she spent the early hours on an Internet forum where young Egyptians anonymously shared their anxieties—and what most of them were anxious about was sex. *How come a guy can do whatever he wants and no one will ever know about it, but not a girl?* she continued. *I don't want to feel like women are victims because of course Allah is just, but why?*

She sat back, cross-legged in her pink pajamas, and waited. Once again, she thanked God for the Internet, because it was a question that couldn't easily be asked offline. Nayera was twenty-four, like all her friends she had never had sex, and sources of information about it were in short supply. "When it comes to these things, there's no discussion," her usually placid mother snapped when she tried to talk to her. "It's a closed subject."

When Nayera's mother married in Cairo in the 1980s, things had been as straightforward as they still seemed in Amal's village. Even among the middle classes, the first generation of a family to move to the big cities and attend university, like Nayera's mother, brought the traditional ideas of the countryside with them. When a young person reached the allotted age—early twenties for women and later twenties for men—their parents simply arranged an alliance with a family of the same religion, level of education, wealth and social class. Sex was something a *bint el-nas*—a well-brought-up girl—learned about after the wedding, in the due course of pleasing her husband and producing children.

For Nayera things were more complicated. However well off their families, Cairo's twenty-first-century twenty-somethings still inhabited a world of arranged marriages, dowries, virginity, filial obedience and religious obligation. But the old rules were only part of the story. Her generation had grown up with Internet porn, Hollywood rom-coms, women's magazines, illicit nightclubs, mobile phones and social-media flirtations. They'd also grown up with the revival of conservative Islam, the spread of headscarves and prayer bruises—marks sported by men who pressed their foreheads ostentatiously hard to the ground in worship—sexual harassment and mass unemployment.

All these currents collided in the world of relationships and marriage. The confusion was driving young people crazy. Many took the path of least resistance, acquiescing meekly or reluctantly to tradition and their families' demands. Others, like Nayera, were trying to find their own way to reconcile all the contradictions. Her mother didn't know that, in secret, her daughter thought about sex and dated men and dreamed of finding someone she could truly love, or struggled with the double standards of a society in which the burden of "purity" fell on girls alone.

When I met Nayera through a mutual friend, she looked to me like the perfect, glossy model of a liberal woman. She wore her dark hair flowing loose and she had a well-paid job in human resources with a multinational food company whose giant fluorescent hotdogs loomed on billboards over Cairo's highways. Like all her friends, she tried hard to be an obedient daughter and, unlike some of them, a faithful Muslim. But she was seething with frustration. She was far franker about its causes than many of the young women I met, who giggled and blushed at the mere mention of anything "impolite." Their coyness enraged her even more.

"For us, sex is the last red line," she said, and grimaced. "The only time it would ever be mentioned in a family like mine is if a girl is getting married. Then her mother might give her some advice."

"What kind of advice?" I asked. Right before the wedding seemed late in the day, but surely this would be the time for reassurance.

Nayera rolled her eyes dismissively. "Nothing! Ridiculous, retarded stuff," she said. "I've never heard of a mother telling her daughter something useful, like make sure you are very clean. Or about contraception. Listen, this is what they tell us: 'On the wedding night, you have to drink a glass of milk before you go to bed. You need energy, you need to be strong for this, because it will be a long night. Then you must put a towel or a small sheet—anything white—underneath yourself to catch the blood. When everything is over, fold it up and put it by the side of the bed. The next day, you must take it to your in-laws' house, and show it around the family, to prove you were a virgin.'"

Nayera laughed at my surprise, her cheeks glowing with exasperation. "My God, can you believe this!" she said. "This isn't even religion, it's village traditions that have survived in the city. This is what happened to my aunt: two years ago, my uncle got married again, to a much younger woman. During the wedding night there was no blood, not because she wasn't a virgin but because her hymen had been broken by sports or accident or whatever. So first thing next morning he marched her to the doctor and demanded 'Why didn't the blood come?' I told her—you're so stupid, you should have cut your wrist and wiped it on the sheet. They just want blood, any blood will do!"

Officially—as far as parents, religious authorities and the state were concerned—for Nayera's generation sex outside marriage remained unthinkable. It was taboo for both Christians and Muslims, rich and poor, city- and country-dwellers. It was illegal for unmarried couples to share a hotel room or rent an apartment, the only private space for those who lived with their families. But in practice, extramarital sex happened more than anyone would admit. Men, especially, had some latitude. Even the law stated that if they were caught with a "prostitute"—a usefully elastic term that could be stretched to cover most women—they became a witness to her crime rather than being charged themselves. For a woman, if she was found out, premarital sex would render her effectively unmarriageable. A great teetering edifice of etiquette and tradition was dedicated to preventing it—or rather, to preventing the appearance that any woman might have had the opportunity to do it.

I was used to thinking of sex between consenting adults as a private act, but in Egypt it was a potential public disgrace. The fear of 'ayb—a word that means "shame" but carries a far more toxic loading—ruled supreme, and a girl's reputation was her and her family's only protection against it. The restrictions varied according to class and where a family lived, but 'ayb could befall any girl at any time, for a hundred reasons—from being seen with a strange man in public to coming home too late, wearing something a little too eye-catching or doing something reserved for men like swearing or smoking or lingering on the street.

31

What all these reasons had in common—as I had found out when I first arrived in Cairo—was the watchful eyes that permanently surrounded you, waiting for a slip. God, for both Muslims and Christians, was the supreme witness, His angels and demons always on hand to record or encourage your sins. But *'ayb* didn't apply exclusively to believers. Egypt's handful of atheists suffered from its effects as much as anyone else, because the responsibility for moral surveillance flowed down from the supernatural realm in a pyramid—to family, friends, colleagues, neighbours, passersby, waiters, shopkeepers and most of all the apartment-building doormen-porters-guards called *bawab*s, the eyes and ears of Cairo.

*Bawab*s were working-class men often brought as children by the buildings' richer owners from their own ancestral villages to the city. They lived with their families in dank basements or cramped rooms under the central stairs, supported by a small monthly fee from each apartment's owner or tenant, topped up with tips for extra services and, often, bribes for the information only they were privy to. *Bawab*s' first loyalty was to the building's owner, who they kept provided with gossip about tenants and neighbors. But the regime also made use of them as informants on foreigners, activists, gay men, prostitutes and anyone else of interest to the security services. Residents who felt themselves at risk could pay for a *bawab*'s silence, but always in the knowledge that a threat or a larger bribe might reverse it. Women were especially vulnerable, because a *bawab* could and would inform not only his fellow *bawab*s but also parents, neighbors and landlords about any minor infraction, leaving a girl's reputation—and therefore her family's—in tatters.

"It's all to protect girls, because they are more precious than men," everyone shrugged when Nayera complained about the double standards that curbed her freedom.

People joked about their symbiotic relationships with their *bawabs*. But to me the web of observation and judgment that stretched between *bawabs*, owners, tenants and neighbors seemed a sinister informal extension of the state's sprawling surveillance machine. Egypt's security services had been consolidated in the 1950s by Gamal Abdel Nasser with the help of a motley international assortment of spies and torturers, including fugitive Nazis he installed in luxury villas and kept working for low pay with the threat of extradition to Israel.[7] Under Mubarak they were estimated to employ 2 million people, dwarfing the armed forces.[8] The largest service, the interior ministry's Amn el-Dawla, state security, monitored not only citizens' political tendencies but their sex lives for any hint of deviation from the state-sanctioned norm that might leave them open to blackmail or prosecution.

Authoritarian politics and the patriarchy were so entwined that I thought political change, if it ever came, must bring Egyptians greater liberties in their private lives too. Or, on the other hand, a loosening of the matrix of social scrutiny might start to unravel more formal mechanisms of political control. It would certainly blunt one of the state's most potent tools for turning Egyptians against each other.

But for the moment, in the mid-2000s, neither looked at all likely. The surveillance hadn't prevented Cairo, at street level, from boiling with sexual frustration. Harassment was a fact of daily life, a constant dispiriting backdrop to moving around the city. On the way to see Nayera, I walked out of my apartment building in Mohandiseen onto the main road nearby, its traffic snarled to immobility under a haze of heat and exhaust fumes. I passed an ambulance stuck with its siren on and the driver leaning sporadically on the horn. As I walked by, he leaned out of the window to tap ash off his cigarette and shout "*Moza, moza!*"—"Hot girl!" A bus driver in the next lane chipped in with an obscene gesture. The remainder of the street was a gauntlet of stares and shouted or whispered threats and propositions in Arabic or broken English: *You are so beautiful*; *You want a real man?*; *I love you fuck you.* Often, it was just someone groping me as I passed through the metro turnstiles, rode a public bus or waited for a taxi. The previous week, walking over a Nile bridge at midday, I was pinned to the railings by a thin young man who crept up behind me under cover of the traffic noise and grabbed me between the legs as drivers and passersby stared on impassively. On the streets I skirted the police and, when I saw them, soldiers and the skinny black-clad conscripts of the riot police, because they would shout and leer as much as anyone else.

Survey after survey found that virtually all Egyptian women reported experiencing sexual harassment. Analysts blamed Egypt's rapidly growing population, overcrowding, rural migration to the cities, social fragmentation, unemployment and, most of all, the soaring cost of marriage that kept many young men single into their late twenties or even thirties. Men who were surveyed blamed women for being inappropriately dressed—a difficult feat when virtually all now wore the headscarf—going out without male protection, or "acting like they wanted it." But when I looked at the hostile, sneering expressions of the men who accosted me on the street I also saw people made powerless in their everyday lives, looking for anyone more vulnerable on whom to take out their anger and frustration.

Eventually, harassment escalated so far that the media began to use the word "epidemic" and the authorities had to acknowledge it. In 2007, women-only carriages were introduced on metro trains. But the young women I knew who could afford it preferred not to travel on public transport or even by taxi, relying instead on their parents or brothers for lifts. The few who had their own cars, like Amal, would move about the city with the windows wound up, doors locked, air conditioning and music on, safely cocooned from the chaos, pollution and men outside. I found it hard to understand how they could accept these restrictions on their freedom, but I saw their resignation was pragmatic. My own handful of attempts to shout down or shame harassers had attracted nothing but abuse, threats of violence and a hostile staring crowd.

Nayera's parents told her the rules they laid down for her were solely for her protection against the ruthless men who waited beyond the front door, and in some ways she knew she had more freedom than many of her friends. She wasn't allowed to move out of the family home, wear tops that showed her arms above the elbow, travel to Egypt's beach resorts unsupervised, or date men. But she could socialize in a mixed group, wear clothes a little tighter or more colorful than her friends', and go out in the evening until 10 p.m. Many of her friends' parents wouldn't let their adult daughters have male friends, wear anything other than conservative clothes or stay out past 9 p.m. These girls were forced into compliance or, more usually, an exhausting double life.

Unfortunately, at least in Nayera's eyes, society believed there was a simple way to monitor girls' behavior—the hymen. Virginity tests might be scientifically dubious, but if a woman didn't bleed on her wedding night, divorce or abandonment, and terminal shame for her family, could easily result. Fear and superstition about the hymen abounded. Girls were afraid to play sports, ride bikes or use the imported tampons that a few supermarkets in Cairo stocked. Nayera's best friend was terrified to shower during her period in case water and blood somehow combined to *burst it right open*, as her mother had balefully warned her could happen. Nayera kept telling her she was about 85% sure this was impossible, but it didn't make any difference.

If a bride feared she might not bleed, there was a long tradition of local folk solutions—the most favored being the tactical insertion of a fresh pigeon giblet. The more modern version was a Chinese-made pouch containing a few drops of food-grade red dye. *Add in a few moans and groans, you will pass through undetectable*, promised the vendors,[9] which provoked a heated parliamentary debate on the decline of Egyptian women's morals. Hymen repair operations offered by discreet clinics across Cairo ranged from a single stitch across the vaginal opening to procedures that cost up to $200 (LE2,000).[10] When one of Nayera's friends, at fifteen, had slipped on the beam in gymnastics practice, her family had dragged the weeping girl to a clinic to be "repaired." Nayera had shuddered at the idea of the same happening to her.

As Nayera waited, one by one, replies to her post started popping up onscreen.

"The hymen's a myth. Find a guy who knows what he's doing and I guarantee you no bleeding will happen," wrote a young man with a trendy spiky hairdo and mirrored aviators.

"It's a test. Like if I told you 'Would you steal a million dollars if no one were to find out?' Allah gave it to you so that you can think a hundred times before you give up something so valuable. Just accept it," wrote a girl.

"It exists because a girl can't tolerate having more than one man in her life. But a man can sleep with you today and her tomorrow with no problem," wrote another guy, who looked quite nice.

Nayera sighed again. This was what she was afraid of. She had long realized that dealing with potential husbands required subtle theatrical skills. Appearing too eager—or, worse, experienced—was a potential disaster. Playing the role of the sweet, naive girl drove Nayera crazy with frustration, and she didn't know what to do about a date she had arranged for the next day with Abdel Rahman, a friend of a friend. She decided to pray *istikhara*, the prayer the Prophet had recommended to Muslims who needed guidance to make a decision, from what job to take to who to marry.

You have power, I have none. And You know, I know not. You are the Knower of hidden things. O Allah, if in Your knowledge, this matter is good for me both in this world and in the hereafter, then ordain it for me, make it easy for me, and bless it for me, she prayed. By the time she had finished, she felt better, and slept.

At 7 p.m. the next day Nayera was waiting for Abdel Rahman in a fashionable outdoor cafe. Thursday night, the start of the Egyptian weekend, was the city's unofficial date night, and the cafe was full of young couples gazing at each other and holding hands when they thought the waiters weren't watching. Nayera felt sick with nerves. Would this finally be the ideal man, religious but open-minded, responsible but fun, who she could marry? The fear of becoming an 'anis—a spinster—struck chill into her heart.[11] Once an unmarried woman reached thirty, the word hung over her head like a neon warning sign and her value in the marriage market plummeted.

She glanced around anxiously. She had agreed to meet Abdel Rahman on the opposite side of the city from their own homes, where they were less likely to be seen by friends, colleagues or meddling relatives. Dating didn't officially exist in the minds of either Egyptian parents or Egyptian society. In upmarket cafes and restaurants customers were under watch from the staff. Upmarket malls had signs warning "No Dating." So in the evenings couples lined the bridges over the Nile, turning their backs to the lanes of traffic. The river was full of garbage, and egrets foraged in the plastic bags and bottles at its margins, but it was the only place in the city where eyes wouldn't be on their faces. In al-Azhar park, one of the city's few fragments of green space, uniformed security guards patrolled the grassy banks overlooking the minarets of the medieval city, rustling the bushes with their batons to check for couples stealing a kiss or holding hands. To the richer couples, they were polite. "You can't sit here in the evening, sir." To the poorer, they were blunt. "What are you doing? This is disgusting! Does her father know about this?"

Abdel Rahman was twenty-nine, a tall, elegantly scruffy news photographer with a Marlboro permanently attached to his long slender fingers. As he smiled at Nayera and sat down, he could see she was nervous. He automatically began telling her stories about his adventures with his camera—shooting gun-runners in the wild tribal villages of southern Egypt, labor strikes in the tough working-class suburbs of Suez, celebrities in the luxury resorts along the Red Sea. Listening to him, Nayera relaxed and started to feel optimistic. He seemed confident, glamorous and clever.

But while he talked and tapped out fresh Marlboros and heard her laugh or gasp admiringly in all the right places, Abdel Rahman's mind was busy elsewhere. He was also anxious. Despite his carefully polished exterior, he had grown up in a village in southern Egypt, where life was still governed by strict clan tradition. The local saying was *el-tar walla el-'ar*, revenge is better than disgrace. Unrelated boys and girls were forbidden from talking together—even the suspicion of an illicit relationship could cause a blood vendetta between clans that could last for fifty years of tit-for-tat murders.

The most important thing, Abdel Rahman's parents had drummed into him from the time he could walk, was to be a man—and to make sure everyone else knew you were one.

"*Khalik geda'a*, be a real man, and don't cry!" his mother admonished him when he fell and skinned his knees.

"*Isteragel*, man up, and fight back! A man takes his rights by force," his father told him when he came home from school tearful over a group of older boys who bullied him in the playground. His father's two favorite words, which Abdel Rahman heard tens of times a day, were *rugoula*, manliness, and *dakar*, a macho man. Slowly his son learned to act them out. Abdel Rahman felt proud when first his sisters, then, as he grew taller and stronger, his mother too, deferred to him. He enjoyed being their guardian, watching over their safety and their morals from his vantage point of strong, rational manliness. He knew that one day he would be leading, supporting and protecting his own wife and children and—quite possibly—his aging parents and unmarried sisters too.

As he grew into a teenager, he found out that part of being a real man was talking about girls. This was one of the more confusing of the tightropes society wanted him to walk—to be both respectable and macho. Abdel Rahman and his friends had no opportunity to even touch a girl's hand, but when the school week started each Sunday they hinted smugly to each other about the "adventures" of the weekend. They muttered respectfully about a Hadith, a saying of the Prophet Muhammad, that intimated—at least in their interpretation—that the Prophet was capable of sleeping with all eleven of his wives in one night. Islam, they learned, was unabashedly frank about sex—for believers' guidance, Hadiths described minute details of the Prophet's relations with his wives and pronouncements on them, and scholars issued fatwas—Islamic legal opinions—on the minutiae of sex acts that could be enjoyed by married couples. But beyond the books of scholarship, there was little equality between men and women. A man who slept with many women was known admiringly as a *nims*, a mongoose, for his cunning. A woman who slept with many men—if such a thing existed, Abdel Rahman could hardly imagine it—was simply a *sharmouta*, a whore.

It was not surprising that the same distinction was drawn by the state in, among others, adultery laws, because the national identity promoted since the military takeover of the 1950s was founded on masculinity. The army was the ultimate expression of virile, dominant Egyptian manliness, and to ensure its values were thoroughly inculcated in the citizenry, all young men underwent compulsory military service. Presiding over the whole scene, in airbrushed official portraits on billboards and government office walls, was the authoritarian father figure of the leader and head of the armed forces—first Nasser, then Sadat and now Mubarak.

The flipside of the reverence for tough men was a state-sanctioned horror of homosexuality and effeminacy. In the playground Abdel Rahman had learned the worst insults you could say to a man—*khawal*, faggot, and *mokhanas*, sissy. The state periodically cracked down on gay men and transsexuals—in the official imagination gay women didn't exist—rounding them up in brutal and well-publicized raids that reinforced the police's image as the alpha males on the street. Because being a "passive" partner was held to be so shameful, even heterosexual men detained by the police or security services could face sexual abuse or rape— sometimes filmed to facilitate later blackmail. Such threats and the fear of being thought unmanly kept most men locked in their macho roles. But even without the state's threat of physical violence, there was plenty to challenge their self-image as powerful providers. Unemployment, menial jobs, political exclusion and endless humiliating encounters with corruption chipped away at the confidence of all but the richest and most powerful.

Remembering his parents' exhortations, Abdel Rahman resolved to always be a real man. In 2001, he arrived at university in Cairo. For the first time, he and his friends from home had the chance to mix with women their own age, and they couldn't believe their luck. The air was full of romance. A few reckless couples had *urfi* marriages—a private, informal agreement that gave their relationship a veneer of religious legitimacy. But the risks for the girls were huge—if they got pregnant or news of the *urfi* marriage got out, they would be ruined.

Avoiding all this, Abdel Rahman wrote romantic poems to a tiny huge-eyed girl in his photojournalism class called Hanan. He knew they would be together forever, as happy as his parents' generation were unhappy, struggling under the weight of their outdated traditions and expectations. Then reality hit. All around him college romances were crumbling, his friends' rainbow bubbles burst by protective families. Most marriages were still formally arranged *gawaz el-salonat*, "living-room marriages," where prospective candidates were identified by trusted matchmakers and paraded before each other while the families looked on. Even "love matches" had to be approved by both families. There was no tradition of a romantic marriage proposal from a man to a woman— instead, the would-be groom took his proposal to the bride's father. And there was no way any father would accept a fresh graduate with no property, no savings, no influence and a modest income.

"Look son, do you have any idea how much my daughter's lifestyle costs per year?" Hanan's father asked Abdel Rahman, not unkindly, when he plucked up the courage to go to the family villa in an expensive suburb of Cairo. According to tradition his parents should have accompanied him, but they were at home in southern Egypt and he was too shy to tell them about Hanan, so he went alone in a cheap shiny suit he'd bought for his graduation ceremony. "You're just a baby—you couldn't even afford to pay for her makeup and handbags," Hanan's father continued. "There's no way I'm giving her to someone like you." After that, Hanan began to avoid him.

"I have to obey my father," she sobbed—but Abdel Rahman was privately sure she'd realized she couldn't handle a life of even relative and temporary poverty.

His bitterness over Hanan ended Abdel Rahman's romantic dreams of marriage. Like his friends, he had grown up watching Western porn, first at illicit video parties, then online, and he realized that the whole world wasn't like Egypt. After he graduated and got a job at a newspaper, he met a string of European girls who smuggled him past suspicious *bawab*s to drink, smoke hash and have sex. For spring and autumn holidays he traveled to Sharm el-Sheikh in Sinai, the pressure valve of Egyptian society, where everything went—if you could afford it. For a young single man with a little money, living away from home, it was a new world. Abdel Rahman came face-to-face with young prostitutes from villages in Ukraine and Belarus, older European holidaymakers on the hunt for handsome young locals, nightclubs that flew in DJs from Ibiza or New York, drugs and wild parties.

For a few years, it was fun. But as he neared thirty, it started to feel empty. He felt guilty and stressed when he thought about the drugs, parties and one-night stands. He knew that even his friends would judge him as a bad Muslim and an irresponsible son. *In Sharm el-Sheikh I'm just an animal, living like all the other animals*, he thought.

"Why isn't he married—is there something wrong with him?" relatives whispered to his parents at family occasions. The covert speculation—*Is he impotent? Is he mentally unstable? Is he, God forbid, one of those perverts who do things with men?*—drove Abdel Rahman crazy.

He realized he had to change. For years, Abdel Rahman hadn't paid much attention to religion. Now he began to listen to Quranic recitation as he stop-started through the choking Cairo traffic to and from work every day. It made him feel calm. He started to pray—at first sporadically, then five times a day. He went to the mosque on Fridays, sitting dutifully cross-legged to listen to the sheikh talk about the torments or bliss of the afterlife. He started to feel a new sense of purpose. He started to think his family were right—it was time for him to marry someone who'd make a home, bring up dutiful children and respect him.

Looking at Nayera, he suspected it might not be her. He maneuvred the conversation around to dating, keeping his tone light.

"This is fun—have you done this before?"

Nayera's heart sank. She knew that there were two categories of men. The first was those who would never, ever accept a girl with a "past." The second was those who appeared open-minded at first, but later on would ask questions. *Have you ever dated someone before me? Did you do anything with him? What happened exactly? Where did he touch you? How many times?* They wanted to know all the details, and then they resented them. Some men even refused to consider girls who'd had arranged engagements that had been broken off.

"Not really," she said, blushing becomingly. Irritation rose within her. *Islam says both men and women should be virgins until marriage*, she thought to herself. *Am I asking him if he's dated anyone, even if he's slept with anyone? Look at him, of course he has!* But she lowered her eyelashes. "I'm quite a conservative person," she murmured. Abdel Rahman looked at her and smiled.

"Of course you are," he said courteously. He paid the bill and drove her home, as a real man should. But as she expected, he did not call her again.

It was easy for me to feel sympathy for young women struggling with dating and marriage, far less so for the men who they complained about. But when I met Abdel Rahman after his date with Nayera, I started to understand the pressures that even the most modern young men were under to demonstrate their manliness and treat women according to traditional codes—and the loss of respect from both men and women if they failed to do so. By the time I met Abdel Rahman, all he could think about was securing a bride. He swung into a once-grand, now down-at-heel Cairo tearoom with another mutual friend, pulled out his usual pack of Marlboros and explained to us the list of qualities he wanted in a wife.

"She must be one, beautiful," he said, exhaling an emphatic blast of smoke and gesturing the numbered points with stabs of his cigarette, "two, religious, three, respectable."

"What do those words mean?" I asked.

"I'll tell you," he said, and I settled back in my chair to listen. In Egyptian Arabic this phrase usually heralds a deeply felt monologue. "First, 'beautiful.' I admit that might be relative, but 'religious' and 'respectable' are not. 'Religious' is a must, because I've seen a lot of immoral stuff. I don't want my wife to be like that." His face wrinkled with distaste at the thought. "'Respectable' means that she shouldn't ever have had a relationship before me, even just dating someone. I don't want any comparison between me and someone else. If she had loved someone before, she might still be thinking of him after we were married, and how would I even know?" He raised his eyebrows expressively at us. "Arab men are jealous by nature—that's just the way we are," he continued. "I want something new which belongs just to me."

"But you've dated girls, and partied in the resorts, haven't you?" I asked. I felt I had to challenge what sounded like hypocrisy. But Abdel Rahman saw things differently. In repeating these received opinions, his confidence was buoyed by knowing that society entirely supported him. Only a handful of Westernized liberals might disagree, and he had left them behind when he left Sharm el-Sheikh.

"Men like me who've done this stuff think like this more than anyone else," he said matter-of-factly. "We know what girls are really like, what they get up to in secret. Yes, I partied, and I lived like a Westerner, and I look back on those days with disgust." He shuddered to emphasize his point. "After all my experiences, I've realized that the personality of the Egyptian man tends to stability. Religion is important, marriage is important, who you marry is important. You have to think—this is the one, this will be the mother of my kids. I don't want her to have done any of this bad stuff. She must be perfect." He stubbed out his last cigarette with a flourish. He looked relieved. "Now," he said, "I'm going to call my relatives."

Two weeks later, they had found a girl whose family had moved to the city from his own ancestral village.

"She's nineteen, and she's never had a chance to mix with men or do anything bad," her father explained. "She was engaged before—but it was arranged with a man she didn't know, whose parents insisted on breaking off the engagement." Abdel Rahman felt this was acceptable, but to secure the engagement he had to endure the traditional visit to his intended's family home. The following morning, his mother had a phone call—the family had provisionally accepted him. At the next meeting, they would get down to the real business of marriage, the precise details of the financial agreement between the families.

The next time I saw Abdel Rahman, he was despondent. Even his exuberant hair drooped dejectedly as he slung himself into a cafe chair.

"What's the problem?" I asked.

He slumped even further. "It's like the Camp David negotiations, haggling between the families about money. I'm not a bridegroom, I'm just a walking bank account," he said. "Brides' families demand so much stuff—what people call 'the list.'" He began to recite from memory, his voice edged with sarcasm. "Apartment—it has to be bought not rented, of course—in a good area. Furniture for the apartment. A car—which has to be a foreign model less than three years old. *Shabka*—that's jewelry for the bride—three rings, one plain gold band, one decorated wedding ring and one large diamond. To the value of $5,000 (LE50,000). *Mahr*—that's money I have to pay to my wife at the wedding, it's an Islamic requirement. Wedding party, in a five-star hotel in Cairo. Honeymoon, a week in a five-star hotel on the Red Sea." He looked up, brightening slightly. "At least I got away with a honeymoon in Egypt. Some people had to take their wives to Paris or Thailand."

The problem of money made Abdel Rahman, for the first time, dissatisfied with tradition—now he felt he was on the wrong end of it.

"All the burden falls on men. Of course we feel angry with girls that we're expected to pay for everything," he said. "They're bankrupting us. Girls don't care, they want everything regardless of how much it costs." He stubbed out his final Marlboro and sat staring into the dregs of his coffee cup. "All couples are fighting about this."

When I got home it was late and I sat on the balcony of my apartment with the lights off, propping my feet on the railing to catch the nighttime breeze and listening to the *bawabs* gossiping cheerfully on their street-side bench two stories below. I thought about Abdel Rahman and Amal. They had come from similar places, rural villages cut off from the big cities and governed entirely by tradition, where young people were taught their aspirations should stretch only to replicating their parents' lives—with more money, if possible.

Amal had completely shattered this mold. With none of the opportunities of a middle-class city girl like Nayera; without the degree in medicine or engineering that was an approved route to status and fortune in Egypt; and despite the opposition of her family and the state, she had made herself into a self-sufficient, financially independent woman with a modern international career. She had openly defied the thousand restrictions and social judgments that kept Nayera zigzagging anxiously between compliance and rebellion. But it had come at the price of the reputation that alone allowed a woman to be accepted in Egyptian society. Having heard his views on the proper role of women, I knew that even an educated man like Abdel Rahman would consider Amal at minimum "not respectable," and probably much worse.

Her financial independence posed a threat to the entire hierarchy of power ingrained by the regime, encouraged by conservative religion, policed by society and reinforced by resentment of the West. In 2002 a large-scale UN report had identified the lack of women's economic and political empowerment as one of the three key areas—along with a lack of freedom and a lack of access to knowledge—holding the Arab world back.[12] The Egyptian state had done much to improve women's access to education—the numbers of men and women in higher education were nearly equal[13]—but relatively little to encourage equality, and much to frustrate it, afterward. Creating a fairer balance between men and women would do little to serve the military men in power.

At first I had been bewildered that young people who wanted modern jobs, modern entertainment and modern conveniences might choose to cling to traditional beliefs about gender roles, sex and marriage. Why would they not want greater personal freedom? But now I could see how difficult it was for anyone, man or woman, to break out of the role assigned to them, and why Abdel Rahman, after his adventures in Sharm el-Sheikh, was reverting to the comfort and certainty of the status quo. In marrying the powerless young woman Amal should have been, his choices would be endorsed by his family, society and the state. Abdel Rahman, Nayera and Amal showed that a few were willing to openly defy the pressures on them and some found ways to subvert them. But many complied, fearful and unwilling to pay the price of challenging power. Overturning a hierarchy was hard, and the results were uncertain. It was a lesson that would apply equally to challenging the state itself.

2

Amr:
Kicking Against a Secret State

Ten years before the revolution, the people who would unite in January 2011 were alone. The state had made sure they had no chance to come together. Amr spent that winter in the run-down cafes that lined Alexandria's seafront, watching scrappy local football on their flickering old TVs or staring at the gray sea with a glass of tea cooling untouched in front of him. He had lived all his twenty-one years in Alexandria and he was bored and angry. He was a heavyset computer-science student with unruly hair and dark eyes that narrowed sardonically at the corners, and his classmates kept a respectful distance from him. Teasing, they called after him: "Hey, lone wolf!"

In spring 2002, the monotony of his days was broken. Amr arrived at college to find thousands of students banded together outside the faculty buildings, hunched against the spring wind whipping in off the Mediterranean. Beyond the campus gates waited rows of riot police with scuffed black helmets and long batons, ready to attack the protest if it grew. They were the same age as the students—underfed, barely educated conscripts from the villages of rural Egypt, bussed in from their barracks in windowless metal vans like shipping containers. Their faces were twisted with resentment; for most of them, it was the closest they would ever come to a university. In the center of Alexandria, their colleagues had just shot dead the first protester of Generation Revolution, a business student a year younger than Amr.

"Palestine will be free!" the students were chanting. "Remember Khaybar, you Jews. Muhammad's army will return!" Amr, jostled in the crowd, started to shout with them, his heart pounding with surprise and exhilaration. The tiny space of rebellion felt electric, because his university was policed by state security, his lecturers vetted by the state and public gatherings of more than five people were banned.[1] It was the first time any of them had publicly defied the rules that bounded their lives. But still no one chanted against the regime.[2] Even the boldest, the romantic young men who wore Palestinian scarves and spellbound girls with talk of being freedom fighters, shouted only "Send us to Sinai to fight the Israelis!" or "Cancel the peace treaty!"

The power of the regime that ruled them was based on keeping their sense of possibility and solidarity in check. Amr had never heard a voice raised publicly against the president, Hosni Mubarak. But Palestine was a cause that united Egypt— an outlet both for anger against Israel and its Western sponsors, and for every other frustration that sprang from living in a corrupt, impoverished military state. Fear and hatred of Israel as a state and anti-Semitism in general was cultivated by the regime, even after the peace treaty of 1979—as long as Egyptians were protesting about Jerusalem and Ramallah, the logic ran, they weren't protesting about Cairo and Alexandria.

Israel was ostensibly Egypt's existential enemy, its opponent in the wars of 1967 and 1973, and the army's raison d'être. In reality, the peace treaty had brought lucrative high-level contacts with it. Egyptian intelligence and army officers had grown hugely rich on deals supplying oil and gas to energy-poor Israel at preferential rates, and the countries' intelligence agencies worked closely together. The treaty also paid for the army and regime—the $1.5 billion it received annually from the United States for maintaining peace had paid for its entire military-security complex.

But the students were only dimly aware of these facts and their anger was bolstered by a sense of divine justification. Like most Muslim men in Egypt, Amr had gone dutifully to the mosque for noon prayers every Friday since he was small. Sitting cross-legged on the scratchy plastic matting while fans whirred overhead, he heard again and again about the importance of liberating Jerusalem and the mosque of el-Aqsa at its heart. The imams exhorted them to remember Khaybar, a Jewish town in Arabia which Muhammad and his army had conquered in the seventh century. For the nine-tenths of Egyptians who were Muslim, the ideas were so ingrained that when the students wanted to chant against Israel's twenty-first-century injustices, Khaybar came automatically to their minds.

Amr lived with his mother, father and younger brother in the once-elegant district of Glimonopolo, where old blue trams rattled along the tracks and the streets sloped down to the sea. Ten days earlier, on the satellite TV news, they had watched Israeli tanks, bulldozers and helicopter gunships attack Palestinian towns in Ariel Sharon's campaign to crush the second intifada, or uprising.

Amr's mother, gentle and emotional, was crying. The close-ups of black-clad Palestinian mothers mourning over their dead children tore at her heart.

"Somebody has to do something to help those poor people," she was saying.

Amr's father, a retired senior bureaucrat whose rages were legendary throughout Alexandria, rolled his eyes. "These Palestinian fags!" he shouted. "They sold their land to the Jews, and now they expect us to sort it out for them?" He threw up his hands at the footage of teenagers aiming stones at Israeli tanks, and repeated a sarcastic saying that some people attributed to the former president Anwar Sadat, "We will fight to free Palestine until the last Egyptian soldier."

"It means that—as usual—we're the only ones doing the job," he told his sons. "We Egyptians are the only real men in the whole stinking mess. Not the Palestinians, and not the dirty useless Syrians, who just sit there hoping we'll invade Israel and take the pressure off the Golan Heights."

Like other middle-aged Egyptians, he thought protesting for Palestine—or anything else—was the height of youthful naivety. He had lived through two wars with Israel: the devastating defeat of 1967 and the heavy losses of 1973, which the Egyptian state declared a victory though it had ended with Israeli forces poised sixty miles (a hundred kilometers) from Cairo.[3]

"Kids like you don't know the cost of war," he lectured Amr from the armchair where he held court with the TV remote, his newspaper and his tea. After a career spent barking orders at subordinates, he saw no reason to break the habit when he spoke to his sons. From them, he expected the same deference and unquestioning obedience. "The situation in Palestine might be bad, even the way our state responds to it might be bad," he continued. "But we can't afford another war with Israel now. The only thing to do is wait and prepare ourselves. Jerusalem will be freed eventually."

But Amr was tired of the logic of passivity. Abroad, he thought, it had created only the Palestinian suffering he saw on TV; at home, only stagnation, poverty and frustration. Others felt the same. Tens of thousands of people took to the streets of Alexandria, Cairo and the industrial cities of the Nile Valley. It was the largest protest for a generation. *Hosni Mubarak zay Sharon, nefs el-shakl, nefs el-luwn—* "Hosni Mubarak is just like Sharon—same appearance, same breed," chanted the boldest.[4] But in a country of over 70 million people[5] they were still a minority, and they were still afraid of the police. After a while, the protests petered out.

While Amr was wondering how to deal with the accumulated frustration and boredom of life in Egypt, I was experiencing everything for the first time. I knew that the regime was repressive. When reporters returned to the magazine where I worked with stories of official corruption or police brutality, the editors hesitated over how much they could print. If newspapers didn't self-censor, the government would do it for them—with consequences. I saw the high-sided black metal trucks of the security forces on the streets as I walked to work, and ranks of thin, dark-skinned conscripts surrounding the tiny protests that sometimes sprang up in central Cairo. And I saw the traces of violent opposition: armed police and soldiers at government buildings, and guards with sniffer dogs and long-handled mirrors checking cars for bombs as they entered the big hotels.

But for me, as for most better-off Egyptians, the menace remained below the surface of everyday life. Bored clerks renewed my visa with no questions asked, and no one spied on my apartment or tapped my phone. I was able to explore the country freely, traveling to remote towns on long bus journeys without suffering anything worse than the inevitable harassment doled out to women. My only contact with the army was the soldiers who recorded my presence at each checkpoint— "Got anything?" they called up to the bus driver at roadblocks that loomed out of the dark on desert roads;

"Just a foreign girl," he'd shout back down—and with the police, skirting the trucks full of conscripts who'd shout at me as I passed. I felt far safer from violent crime in central Cairo than I did in London. These were some of the benefits for those who toed the line in a police state.

In those first two years in Egypt, though I studied hard, my Arabic was still stumbling and basic, I was still far from having any true Egyptian friends and I didn't understand the majority of what I saw and heard around me, let alone its tangled context. What really puzzled me was why educated people my own age, graduates in their twenties, seemed to accept the repression. I didn't understand why many not only respected but loved the army. I didn't understand why others shrugged their shoulders at the political status quo. But change was happening beneath the surface, and my arrival coincided with the first public acts of defiance of those who would go on to lead the revolution against Mubarak. Amr and I were the same age. When I got to know him, his story showed how the collision of chance and circumstance could transform an "average" young Egyptian who accepted received ideas about family, religion and the state into someone who was ready to fight for a very different future.

Amr had grown up in a country where time felt like it was standing still. When Mubarak took power in 1981, he had promised Egypt stability after years of turbulence. What it got was stagnation. The military state controlled all potential avenues of dissent, from the toothless opposition parties and the central Islamic institution, al-Azhar, to the handful of broadcast TV channels and even the list of approved clubs university students could join. The army leveraged this stranglehold for profit, its business empire stretching from manufacturing to tourism to major infrastructure projects. Retired officers filled university vice chancellorships and provincial governorships, or ran army-owned oil and gas companies.

The corruption touched everyone, privileged or not, because of *wasta*, the ineffable substance that greased the wheels of every sphere of Egyptian life. *Wasta*—connections to influential individuals who might or might not require favors or bribes in return—could get you a driver's license, no test required; shorten your compulsory military service; get you cut-price travel or a coveted place on the hajj pilgrimage to Mecca; a cheap apartment; a reduced criminal sentence; a place on professional sports teams; or a job, regardless of your qualifications. Senior bureaucrats like Amr's father were constantly surrounded by hangers-on and supplicants hoping to benefit immediately from *wasta* or to cultivate it against future eventualities.

The only consistent challenge to the regime came from the Muslim Brotherhood, the Islamic revival movement founded in 1928 by the schoolteacher Hassan al-Banna. Al-Banna believed that the post–World War I weakness and fragmentation of the Muslim world were symptoms of a spiritual malaise caused by the secular influence of the West. The solution, he argued, was a return to the original values of Islam in all areas of life—a path that would gradually lead to the restoration of a glorious united Islamic state, the caliphate.[6] From its earliest days, poorer Egyptians especially trusted the Brotherhood as pious and incorruptible, calling the Brothers *betou' rabenna*, God's people.

Though Nasser had relied on the Brotherhood's support during his 1952 coup against the British-backed monarchy, when he came to power he turned savagely on his former allies. Two years later, thousands of Brothers were languishing in prisons and desert concentration camps and the movement itself was forced underground. His rivals eliminated or contained by his security services, Nasser set about trying to establish his own secular version of the caliphate—a pan-national United Arab Republic with himself at its head.[7] For a brief while, Egypt was the undisputed leader of the Arab world.

As a young state official in the 1960s, Amr's father had worshipped Nasser. The new state had given him a life his father could never have dreamed of—a way out of his feudal farming village, a modern education and a promising career. But 1967 changed everything. While Nasser issued threats, massed troops in the Sinai and closed the Straits of Tiran to Israeli shipping, the Israelis launched a devastating air strike that destroyed Egypt's air capacity, followed by a ground offensive in the Sinai.

But Egyptian state radio broadcast stirring music and confident proclamations of victory. Egyptian forces had destroyed hundreds of Israeli warplanes, it assured listeners, taken thousands of prisoners and would soon enter Tel Aviv.[8] While citizens celebrated, a low-ranking bureaucrat approached Amr's father at his office in Alexandria, his eyes full of fear.

"Boss, I have to tell you a secret," he said. He led Amr's father to a cheap apartment nearby. In the gloom a young man was lying on the floor, delirious with fever, his feet blackened and hugely swollen. It was the bureaucrat's brother, a soldier who had been sent to fight in Sinai. Two days earlier, when Nasser's field marshal realized the war was lost, he had ordered the troops to retreat from the peninsula any way they could. The soldiers struggled on foot through the desert, hunted by the Israelis, dying of thirst. Thousands were lost. As Amr's father looked down at the soldier, slowly realizing what had happened, his faith in Nasser and his promises shattered.

By the time Anwar Sadat became president in 1970, Arab nationalism had failed. Nasser was dead, Israel was flourishing and Arab states were weakened and humiliated by the defeat. While paying lip service to his predecessor's genius, Sadat purged Nasser's socialist allies, reoriented Egypt away from Russia and toward the West and began to open the economy to foreign investment. At the same time, as a counterweight to his leftist enemies, he released Nasser's Brotherhood prisoners, encouraged religious student groups, cultivated a prominent prayer bruise and styled himself "the believer president." The war of 1973 was hailed as a divine redemption from the socialist catastrophe of 1967—urban legends insisted angels had fought alongside the Egyptian forces, and soldiers had triumphed by shouting *"Allahu Akbar!"* at their Jewish enemies.[9] With the Brotherhood still outlawed, more radical groups sprang up. The shock of his peace treaty with Israel was more than they could accept. On October 6, 1981, a secret cell of jihadi army officers assassinated Sadat at the annual military parade celebrating his so-called victory over Israel in 1973. His vice president Hosni Mubarak, who was himself wounded in the attack, took power.

Ruthlessly crushed after the assassination, by the late 1980s radical groups had begun to regroup in their strongholds along the Nile. Anyone who fell foul of Mubarak's bulwark against them, state security, risked being snatched from their homes and taken to torture cells under government buildings in Cairo or jails in the remote desert. Most Egyptians, terrified of the same thing happening to them, steered as clear of the regime's red lines—political, religious and social—as if they were high-voltage fences. In Syria, Iraq, Libya and Tunisia, Mubarak's fellow dictators had ensured their people felt the same.

*

As the state clamped down around him, for teenage Amr in the 1990s there was nothing to do and nowhere to go. Before the 1952 revolution, Alexandria had been the most cosmopolitan city in Egypt, the business and pleasure capital of Greek, Jewish, Italian and Levantine merchant dynasties. Once Nasser nationalized their businesses and confiscated their assets, they fled. Amr's father and his friends lamented the half-remembered glories of *ayam el-khawagat*, the days of the foreigners, swapping the names of the few prized foreign-trained car mechanics and tailors who remained. Others had no such nostalgia. The gracious colonial villas were being pulled down, and in their place ugly apartment blocks anchored with cheap Romanian steel were mushrooming to house migrants streaming from the villages of the Nile delta.

Alexandria's long history of learning and culture stretched from Euclid to Omar Sharif, but now there was no independent art, music, cinema or theater, and everyone dressed in the same drab, locally made clothes. Amr's generation were growing up in a stifling atmosphere. For teenage Amr and his friends, the intellectual highlight was skipping school to watch soft porn in a cheap cinema where unemployed men masturbated next to them in the darkness and they had a better-than-even chance of being robbed at knifepoint in the toilets. They became connoisseurs of "bikini movies," the racy Egyptian B-movies made to soothe public frustration after the war of 1967, and their successors filmed in Beirut after Sadat had expelled the producers to pacify the Islamists. They weren't explicit, but you could catch glimpses of a starlet in a swimsuit or even, if you were lucky, in her underwear. When the restive male audience screamed abuse during boring dialogue or plot exposition, the managers screened what they called "the important bits"—a spliced-together ten-minute reel of bikini scenes from a dozen different films—to calm them down.

When the cinemas were closed, they sneaked bottles of cheap local gin from the Christian-run liquor stores, and took them down to the seafront in the dark. Hidden among the huge boulders that line the shore, they choked down the foul-tasting spirit that rumor said could leave drinkers brain-damaged or blind. It always made the boys vomit and often they passed out on the sand in their clothes, coming home late and disheveled to their anxious unsuspecting mothers.

Beyond a few American action films, no one had much idea what was going on in the outside world. Though, unlike his monolingual parents, Amr was learning French at his private school, like his friends he had never left Egypt. One neighbor's uncle had emigrated to the United States, and sent his nephew a pair of Nike trainers. Amr and the other boys gathered round, disbelieving, staring at the gleaming sports shoes as if they had fallen from outer space.

"The West must be amazing," said one boy. A silence fell as they tried to envisage it.

"But look at their women—they go round half-naked," said another boy eventually. No one mentioned the bikini movies. They had all seen the scantily clad lovelies who always needed rescuing by Sylvester Stallone or Jean-Claude Van Damme, only to gratefully lavish favors on their deliverer.

"They're sleeping around, doing dirty stuff outside marriage," agreed a third. "Plus it's full of faggots, thank God we don't have them here." They felt comforted by the thought that, in terms of morals and masculinity if not sports shoes, they were undoubtedly superior.

Then came a sound from the outside world. A few kids came to school with cassettes of loud, angry music played by bands with weird names: Metallica, Megadeth, Pantera. Suddenly, all the tough boys who worked in car repair shops, and the more daring middle-class kids, were wearing black T-shirts screenprinted with skulls or pentagrams. Metal was a scream of frustration, a password to a secret world that parents and the state couldn't enter. In the bedroom that he shared with his brother, Amr began blasting out tapes he bought from a shady character called Moharram who claimed he could get you any metal album in the world, no matter how obscure, within seventy-two hours.

The metal fans didn't know it as they gathered in scruffy cafes and sneaked into abandoned old villas to play music and smoke, but state security were watching them too. With their long hair and suspiciously Westernized taste in music, they weren't what real Egyptian men were supposed to look like. The state-controlled tabloids began to print lurid rumors—leaked by the intelligence services—of orgies, drug-taking and black-magic rituals in the derelict mansions of Cairo and Alexandria. Of course, the Israelis were implicated. "Mossad orchestrates Satanic orgies in Egypt," screamed one headline.[10] Seventy-eight teenage metalheads were seized from middle-class homes in Cairo and Alexandria one January dawn in 1997, the secret police upending their bedrooms in the search for tapes and black T-shirts.

At school assembly the next morning, rumors swept the hall. A handful of students in the year above Amr were missing. Others, the boys hissed to each other when the teachers weren't looking, had gone from the most exclusive schools in the city. After two weeks in prison, while their families frantically pulled every official string they could think of, the teenagers were freed.

"Personally, I don't think they worship the Devil," announced the public prosecutor as he released them. "But they are trying to follow the Devil by having sex, drugs and any evil things." A moral panic swept the nation's middle-class families. For once, the enemies of stability and security weren't bearded fundamentalists plotting jihad in the remote desert, but their own children, in the bosom of their polite and civilized homes. Amr's father didn't speak enough English to understand what the metal bands were screaming about, but he read the papers and watched the news and realized his eldest son was a budding diabolist. Along with the families of the other metalheads, he cracked down. Their tapes and T-shirts were confiscated, their modest attempt at rebellion was crushed.

In the end, change came from the direction Amr least expected—above. In 1999, Hosni Mubarak's second son Gamal, a thirty-five-year-old city slicker with a receding hairline and a taste for European designer suits, returned from London determined to change his country. He saw how his father's generation, with their old-fashioned military backgrounds and bone-deep aversion to risk, were running Egypt. To Gamal Mubarak and the coterie of businessmen he gathered around him, the uneducated workforce, outdated industries and vast, lumbering state sector were an embarrassment. Their plan was to transform Egypt into a modern, neoliberal, Western-style economy—without tackling corruption, holding free and fair elections or reining in the security services—with Gamal Mubarak at its head. In 2000 there was an encouraging precedent: thirty-four-year-old Bashar al-Assad inherited the presidency of Syria from his dictator father Hafez. The same year, Gamal was appointed to the general secretariat of his father's National Democratic Party. "Broadening the participation of young people in political life is an essential guarantee of a smooth handover of responsibility from one generation to the next," announced his father.[11] Having always described himself as the father of the nation, he was now lining up his son to follow him.

The priority for Gamal Mubarak's modernization plan, the bluntly named New Thinking, was to get Egypt online. In 2000, less than 1% of Egyptians were connected to the Internet,[12] against over 40% of Americans.[13] Through a series of lucky chances, Amr was one of them. Like all middle-class teenagers, his future had been settled by the dreaded *senawiyya 'ama*, final secondary school exams. Personal preference and aptitude were irrelevant. Students with the highest grades were funneled straight into medical school, those slightly below them into engineering, then commerce, law and finally the despised humanities. Amr, who was aiming to study medicine, endured a two-year marathon of stress, private tuition, long hours of study and extra reading, punctuated by his father's exhortations and threats. When he arrived at the examination center, he saw students' mothers fainting outside the halls, girls weeping hysterically and boys vowing grimly to commit suicide.

His nerves intolerably frayed by the wait to discover his son's destiny, Amr's father used *wasta* to get his results before they were officially released. The family gathered round the paper, his father furious, his mother tearful: 85.5%. To study medicine, Amr would have needed 97.5%. It was just enough to scrape him on to a course in computer engineering at a private university in Alexandria. Luckily, his father didn't insist on funneling him straight into the state bureaucracy using *wasta*, or, worse, forcing him to become a police officer.

By his second year of college, Amr had laid hands on a 56K modem and coaxed an expert friend into helping him install it at home. The modem enraged his father because it tied up the phone line and ran up the bill, so Amr got used to cautiously switching it on late at night, faking coughing fits to cover up the stuttering dial-up sound. It was a sign of things to come. By 2009, a quarter of Egyptians would be online.

But New Thinking had side effects the state had never dreamed of. In a tightly controlled society where public gatherings were banned, the Internet was a free space for young Egyptians to come together without worrying about surveillance from neighbors, state security or parents. In his bedroom, Amr started blogging. *For exchange, secondhand Egyptian citizenship, one responsible owner, only twenty-five years old, for an electric heater or fan,* he wrote. Gradually, he met other bloggers, leftist activists, artists, intellectuals, computer geeks and students who had protested for Palestine and Iraq. In the safety of forums, chatrooms and blogs, they started to talk about all the subjects it was impossible to discuss in real life—social taboos, religion and even political change.

Amr had always thought of himself as a more or less ordinary guy—perhaps a little clever and solitary, but liking football and Lebanese pop starlets, going to smoke shisha in cafes in the evenings and to pray at the mosque on Fridays. He expected his life to unfold in the same way his father's had—graduation, marriage, a stable job and years of supporting his wife and children and looking after his parents. Now, the Internet was starting to unravel all these beliefs. Sitting up all night chatting online, he heard opinions he had never dreamed existed. The most shocking were about faith. Some Christian posters openly criticized Islam. Others declared they didn't believe in any God or any religion. They wanted to be governed not by myths and miracles, they said, but by logic and reason.

At first, Amr was horrified. Even to tread too close to the red lines around Islam—let alone declaring yourself an atheist—was unthinkable. In 1992 the writer Farag Foda had been shot dead by jihadis for satirizing extremist beliefs; two years later the eighty-two-year-old Nobel Prize–winner Naguib Mahfouz was wounded in a similar assassination attempt.[14] Growing up, Islam had been an unquestioned constant: everything around Amr reinforced that he should pray, go to the mosque, fast in Ramadan, believe in God and His Prophet and the Day of Judgment. But now atheism was starting to make more and more sense. The next time he went to the mosque, he arrived late, kicking off his shoes and hurrying to join the line of worshippers. By the time he had finished praying, everyone else had left and another man had stolen his shoes. *It's a sign*, thought Amr furiously, standing in his socks. *From now on, I will be a rational person* wa khalas. *And that's it.*

Just as he thought he was shaking off the old habits of obedience, the regime dragged Amr back. When he graduated in 2003, Amr was called up for military service.

While they might love the army in theory, everyone longed to escape conscription in practice. One of Amr's friends doggedly ate his way to eighty-eight pounds (forty kilos) over his recommended weight in the hope of an exemption. Non-graduates had to serve for three years, so in rural areas some cut off a big toe or, to be extra certain, their right index finger. The army took first pick of the conscripts, followed by the other armed forces. Those left over—usually the poorest, least educated and physically weakest—served in the Central

Security Forces under the interior ministry, where their duties included riot policing. They were the young men who had met the protests at Amr's university.

With his classmates from the engineering faculty, Amr traveled out to the call-up center in the desert outside Alexandria. When they arrived, thousands of half-dressed young men were packed into the hangars, the smell of sweat and fear hanging thickly over them.

"It looks like Judgment Day," said Amr, and his friends nodded mutely, thinking of the panicked resurrected crowds they had all heard preachers describe in their sermons. Soon they too were stripped off and awaiting their medical check. Amr looked down the line of pallid, unfit computer engineers. They were all in traditional white briefs, because they'd inherited from their fathers the idea that colored underwear was fit only for effeminate Westerners. Some were too fat, others were too thin, others wore thick-lensed glasses.

A military intelligence officer strolled along the line of near-naked men, slowly looking them up and down. Amr felt himself wilting. He would take the strongest candidates to be trained as specialist officers, an honor that would extend the period of service from fourteen months to three years. To be selected was everyone's greatest fear.

"You, you and you, come with me," the officer rapped out and strode off, the men scurrying awkwardly after him in their briefs.

For his basic training, Amr was sent to a camp in the desert outside Cairo where misshapen pyramids even older than Giza's loomed over the barracks. Graduate conscripts particularly dreaded it because they were at the mercy of the *zubat el-mekhla*, duffel-bag officers, uneducated professional soldiers who hated their middle-class charges. Other than repetitive physical exercises and fetching cigarettes for the duffel-bag officers, they learned little. There was no evidence of the huge amounts of money and advanced military hardware Egypt received annually from the United States as a quid pro quo for maintaining peace with Israel and allowing U.S. warships priority passage through the Suez Canal.[15] The conscripts shot three bullets over the course of their brief army career, running to collect the empty cartridges because the officers wanted proof that live ammunition would not find its way onto the black market. Looking around him, Amr reflected that three bullets was plenty, because Egypt had enough problems without having every adult male a trained killer.

When basic training ended, the conscripts used every scrap of *wasta* they had to secure an easy posting—anything from selling pickled olives from army farms on a stall in Cairo to redecorating generals' homes or running errands for their wives. One friend of Amr's was posted to an army-owned complex of kitschy themed reception halls to dress up in ancient Egyptian costume and greet wedding guests. The less fortunate toiled as free labor on army construction projects or in army factories, but they didn't care. Anything was better than being posted to the Western Desert to bake in the sun at remote checkpoints, or to the Sinai to be shot at by drug smugglers.

Military service had given Amr a firsthand experience of the waste, corruption and pointlessness of the military bureaucracy. On one home leave, he watched a new round of protests on the TV. Emboldened by the protests of 2002, when the American-led coalition invaded Iraq in March 2003, Egyptians took to the streets and chanted against both the invasion and Mubarak, who had tacitly supported it. The people loved Iraq and Saddam Hussein—in the 1980s hundreds of thousands of Egyptians had lived there as migrant workers and been treated far more generously than they were in Libya or Saudi Arabia. A 140,000-strong government-sponsored "official protest" in Cairo's central stadium, which as a major concession featured speakers from the Muslim Brotherhood, failed to defuse public anger.[16] On March 20, three thousand students, Islamists and leftist activists took control of Tahrir Square, the symbolic heart of Cairo. The next day, thousands more rampaged through downtown Cairo high on adrenaline, showering riot police with stones, defying water cannon and attack dogs. It was a sign that the state was not as invulnerable as it thought.

Despite the minor inconvenience of the protests, as far as the Mubaraks were concerned New Thinking was working perfectly. To speed it along, in 2004 a new cabinet of pro-business technocrats halved the top tax rate. Foreign investment flooded in. For a few years, the economy achieved 7% growth. The IMF and the global business community applauded.[17] The money began to flow—for the few. Western-style shopping malls spread gleaming facades across the smarter districts of Cairo and Alexandria. Miles of newly built luxury villas and compounds sprang up in the desert outside the city and along the Mediterranean and Red Sea coasts. In their enclaves, the wealthy could suddenly find a functioning ATM, buy clothes from Zara, H&M and Marks & Spencer, or Skippy peanut butter, Barilla pasta and Lindt chocolate.

In the years after I arrived in 2003, I could see Cairo was transforming. Alongside foreign investment, the "war on terror" industry was booming. Westerners had started to stream into the city, a cheap base for studying Arabic or commuting to Baghdad, where the coalition was spending billions of dollars in the attempt to subdue Iraq, or Dubai, gateway to the war in Afghanistan. Language schools, apartments in well-heeled districts and expensive restaurants filled up with trainee diplomats, intelligence officers, UN and World Bank officials, think-tank researchers, freelance journalists and hopeful students. I was one of them, a new graduate working on a local newspaper and studying Arabic. Everyone was on the make, financially or otherwise. "Are you interested in working for the British government?" asked an anonymous man in a suit who showed up at my language school one day, primed somehow with all my personal details.

Multinational IT companies were also arriving in Egypt, offering bright graduates salaries irresistible to those raised on their parents' modest state wages. Amr had always believed that he would never leave Alexandria, but by 2005 he was living in a shared apartment in Cairo, working for a Gulf-based software company and slowly getting to grips with the unfathomable jargon and arcane processes of the global corporate world. He was now the modern worker that New Thinking had dreamed of.

At first, the young developers struggled to throw off their deeply ingrained habits of rote learning. Amr thought back to high school, where a question such as "What is your opinion of the nineteenth-century court poet Ahmed Shawqi?" was answered in bullet points, right or wrong, to be checked against a model answer. He knew Ahmed Shawqi was a terrible writer and a shameless sycophant to boot, but he had dutifully regurgitated the received opinion that he was a patriotic genius. Now, that mindset had to be relinquished in favor of exotic American project-management concepts like "agile development," the "waterfall" and the "spiral."

The HR department was busy devising basic training in office attire and etiquette because many of Amr's colleagues were what people teasingly called "genius farmers," young men from provincial universities with rough rural manners and a talent for IT. The genius farmers couldn't believe they were working in a sparkling glass-and-steel building with a cleaning team, a canteen and private buses that took them from their homes to the office. Now doormen and taxi drivers politely addressed them by the title *bashmohandes*, chief engineer. As their status started to rise, so did their dreams.

"By the time we're thirty-something our salary might be half a million Egyptian a year!" a colleague from a delta village told Amr excitedly. "That's $70,000! Life is getting good, man."

"What are you going to do with it?" asked Amr.

"I'll send some money to my mother in the village, to invest in land. Prices per *feddan* are really going up, and I can probably get five *feddan* already!"

The solid middle-class colleagues who were saving to buy apartments in new compounds outside Cairo had their own dreams.

"Now we've got the money sorted, we should all be getting married," said another colleague, winking at Amr. Because sex before marriage was close to impossible, the subject was on everyone's mind almost as much as climbing the social ladder. "And there's no shortage of candidates."

"Oh, you have someone lined up?" Amr knew the young female staff brought homemade breakfasts they blushingly distributed to unmarried senior developers, and the junior developers who they calculated had good prospects. The neatly boxed cheese, falafel and salads showcased their future wifely skills.

"Not a developer, thanks!" said his colleague, grinning. "We know how hard we all work, she'll never be at home to take care of the kids. No, I just want someone ordinary. Then I'll trade in my used car for a new car and I'll really be on my way up."

While the developers' fortunes soared, New Thinking had left nine-tenths of the country behind. They had no stake in Gamal Mubarak's vision of a new Egypt. Food prices were soaring and by 2007 a fifth of Egyptians were unable to meet their basic living needs.[18] The government's aggressive privatization program met with waves of workers' strikes, sit-ins and demonstrations. By 2009 the government claimed that 60% of people aged between fifteen and twenty-nine, and up to the same proportion of new graduates, were unemployed, but no one knew the true totals.[19] Poverty drove poorer young men to desperate measures: 10,000 to 20,000 Egyptians a year were paying human traffickers thousands of dollars to make the dangerous, illegal boat journey to Europe in search of work.[20]

Even in the middle classes, many were locked out of the new prosperity. Graduates without *wasta* or technical skills took low-paid work in cafe chains, as taxi drivers or as bellboys in hotels in Luxor and Sharm el-Sheikh. Others—like Amr's best friend Seif, who worked as an accountant in the ministry of justice—were swallowed by the public sector, which still accounted for a third of regular employment. New Thinking had left this corner of the state untouched. Not only was it not connected to the Internet, Seif's office didn't have a single computer. The fourteen people in his department worked crammed into a single room with their calculators and old-fashioned ledgers. When Seif and Amr drank tea after work at their favorite street cafe, they had to laugh at the gulf between the state's modernizing PR and reality.

*

Offline, Egypt felt as stifled as ever, but online Amr was hearing new ideas and meeting new people every day. Gradually, they started to meet face-to-face too. For decades, Cairo's belle époque downtown neighborhood had been a gathering place for artists and intellectuals. Now, bloggers and software developers were joining the writers, cartoonists, human rights lawyers and leftist activists who sat up all night talking in its scruffy pavement cafes and called themselves *wust el-baladaween*, "downtownists." It was a space where the normal rules of politics, tradition, sex and religion didn't apply—or at least were temporarily suspended. Learning from them, Amr became obsessed with the changes that had swept eastern Europe when he was a boy. Over and over, he watched the video for the Scorpions' song "Wind of Change," with its scenes of the fall of the Berlin Wall. Those communist regimes, seemingly so mighty and permanent, had crumbled. What would it take to create the same change in Egypt?

With a motley assortment of liberals, leftists, Nasserists, Arab nationalists, Trotskyites and even some of the more liberal Muslim Brothers, the downtownists formed a movement called Kefaya, Enough. They began to organize small protests demanding an end to the emergency law, a promise that Gamal Mubarak would not succeed his father and free elections. The United States was also stepping up pressure on its ally for evidence of "democratic reform," and in February 2005 Mubarak announced a referendum on multi-candidate presidential elections—having just made sure to imprison the opposition politician Ayman Nour, his main rival if elections went ahead.

Kefaya stepped up their protests, and the bloggers began carefully documenting cases of police brutality. Human rights organizations had described the use of torture as an "epidemic," spreading from political prisoners to those detained for ordinary crimes. Torture, they found, included "beatings with fists, feet and leather straps, sticks and electric cables; suspension in contorted and painful positions accompanied by beatings; the application of electric shocks; and sexual intimidation and violence."[21] These techniques and Egypt's pliable government also made it a favored destination for extraordinary rendition: during these years Western countries including the United States and Sweden were discovered to have delivered around sixty terror suspects into Egyptian custody.[22]

Suddenly, all Egypt was talking about torture and the blogs. Following Western pressure, Ayman Nour was released to stand against Mubarak. But the supposedly free presidential elections of September 2005—from which external monitors were banned—were a huge disappointment. Ayman Nour won 8% of the vote to Mubarak's 89% and was promptly re-imprisoned.[23] Kefaya began to splinter. As access to the Internet spread, the Egyptian blogosphere was swamped by new bloggers, "most of them doing nothing but trying to find a foreign girlfriend," Amr said scornfully to his friends. By the end of 2007 Amr had begun to think change would never happen, so he left the downtownists talking about art and politics and turned back to his own life.

Then, in summer 2010, a twenty-eight-year-old called Khaled Said was dragged from an Internet cafe and beaten to death by police in Amr's home city of Alexandria.[24] A journalist friend of Amr who lived in the same neighborhood as Khaled Said's family was given a photograph they had taken in the police morgue. Two images of the young man—one clean-cut in a hooded sweatshirt, the other, horribly disfigured after death—spread rapidly across newspapers, TV stations, Facebook and Twitter. Amr was shocked. Police brutality was nothing new, but most middle-class Egyptians had managed to convince themselves that it was something that happened only to the poor, that as long as they stayed clear of politics, they would be safe. Khaled Said's death—offering a window into what went on out of sight in prisons and police stations—showed them that their respectability was no protection. In Dubai, an Egyptian Google executive called Wael Ghonim saw the pictures and set up an anonymous Facebook page he called We Are All Khaled Said. With other social media sites, the page began to organize small-scale protests marking the murder.

Amr's gradual discovery of the Internet, atheism, political activism, the blogs and the free spaces of downtown Cairo had transformed him into an individual who was hungry for freedom and had the knowledge and willpower to fight for it. And now the death of Khaled Said was motivating young Egyptians far beyond the downtownists—liberals, Islamists, Christians, the progressive, the conservative and the politically apathetic alike. At first, at least, they were calling only for a stand against police brutality and for the removal of Habib el-Adly, the hated interior minister. If Mubarak's regime had been craftier, it could have contained the whole thing. But the Tunisian uprising that began in December 2010 and swept away the president Zine al-Abidine Ben Ali on January 14, 2011, fanned the flames. By the time We Are All Khaled Said called for protests on January 25, it was too late for the regime. A generation of young Egyptians was waking up to the desire for freedom.

3

Ayman and Mazen:
Believers on the Path to Paradise

Ayman was sixteen and he was surrounded by hypocrites, dissemblers and false believers. Let alone Hosni Mubarak's regime, which claimed to be Muslim but had no intention of applying the sharia as it was clearly laid down in the Quran and Hadiths, the ordinary Egyptians around him—his school friends, teachers, people on the metro or in the supermarket—weren't true Muslims. The worst of all were his family, with their easygoing, Westernized life in a leafy suburb of Cairo. If his parents didn't want to take a phone call, they would ask Ayman to tell the caller, untruthfully, that they were asleep. They didn't pray all of the five daily prayers. They made fun of women who wore face veils, and men who grew the voluminous beards of the devout. They cared more about worldly success and comfort than about their eternal fate in the afterlife.

Disgusted by the corruption of Egypt in 2004, Ayman looked back to the purity of seventh-century Arabia. He decided he was now a Salafi—a follower of the *salaf*, the first three generations of Muslims. From now on, he would model his thoughts, words and deeds on those of the Prophet, his Companions and those close to them. Everyone around him might be bad, but he could be pure and righteous.

The Salafis were the twenty-first-century face of a movement born in the Arabian peninsula nearly three centuries earlier, when a puritanical preacher called Muhammad ibn Abd al-Wahhab had made a pact with a tribal leader called Muhammad bin Saud. Ibn Abd al-Wahhab would provide spiritual guidance, crushing folk traditions such as venerating saints' shrines and stripping Islam back to what he saw as its fundamentals; Bin Saud, political and military leadership. Their alliance swept the peninsula and laid the foundations of modern Saudi Arabia. Now Salafism, fueled by Saudi oil money, was gaining ground across Muslim communities worldwide—including in Egypt.

Salafi thought underpinned violent movements like al-Qaeda, whose second-in-command was the Egyptian doctor Ayman al-Zawahiri. But most Salafis avoided overt opposition even to unjust governments, preferring to withdraw from the world into their own bubble of moral purity and certainty.

Because of this, Mubarak tolerated their spreading influence—if Egyptians wanted to be devout, better that they become politically passive Salafis than active and organized Muslim Brothers. Though the Brotherhood was still officially banned, its popularity was growing with disgruntled citizens. In the parliamentary elections of 2000, Muslim Brothers standing as independent candidates had managed to win seventeen out of 454 parliamentary seats—more than any other opposition body—despite widespread electoral fraud and police repression.[1] The security services, determined that the Salafis would not muster similar support by stealth, kept them on a short leash with surveillance, detention and torture.

Seeing them persecuted by the cruel, corrupt regime only made Ayman more certain the Salafis were right. He stopped shaking hands with women, even the middle-aged mothers of classmates he had known all his life, because their touch might seduce him. He gave up listening to music because it might awake immoral passions, and taking photographs because he was terrified of committing *shirk*, idolatry. He believed that all women should cover their faces, because the Prophet's wives were said to have done so, and all men should wear an ankle-length robe, because a Hadith stated that any part of a man's lower garment that hung below his ankles would burn in hellfire. His parents forced him to wear his uniform to school, but when he slipped out of the house before dawn for the first prayer he wore a *galabeyya* robe that flapped draughtily around his calves. He promised himself that when the time came he would marry only a devout woman who wore the niqab. Ayman's family were puzzled, but at first they thought it was just a teenage phase.

"So will I ever be able to see my future sister-in-law's face?" asked his younger brother, joking.

"No, of course you won't," snapped Ayman.

Egypt might look godless to Ayman, but from my first disoriented walks around Cairo, I saw and heard how deeply religion was woven into its fabric. At night, green neon glowed from thousands of minarets. The call to prayer wrenched me out of sleep before dawn, suddenly silenced the music in cafes and boomed over the metro PA system. Every morning, tapes of Quranic recitation echoed from taxis, shops, government offices and public buses. Most women covered their heads; many men displayed prayer bruises on their foreheads. Social interaction proceeded by a litany of Islamic formulae, of which the simplest—*inshallah*, God willing—was considered a reasonable answer to everything from "Will my mother survive this surgery?" to "Does this bus stop at the corner?" People of all ages, rich and poor, Muslims and Christians, told me proudly that "Egyptians are religious by nature." Faith wasn't just a private conviction, it was a communal identity reinforced hundreds of times a day through word and deed. Hardly anyone dared—or wanted to—deny it.

In all my twenty-three years of life in the UK, I'd never discussed my religious beliefs or lack of them. In a world bounded by the pragmatic values of effort, ambition and enjoyment, the subject simply never came up. Now I was bombarded with questions about my convictions by colleagues, taxi drivers, shopkeepers and curious strangers in the street. To them it wasn't prying, a concept that anyway had little traction in Egypt, but slotting me into my correct social space—and instantly determining my status in the hereafter.

"So, you're Muslim?" Muslims asked me hopefully.

"So, you're Christian?" Christians asked me even more hopefully. Though Egypt's Christians were mostly Coptic Orthodox—an incense-drenched, icon-venerating denomination that had little in common with the restrained Anglicanism I knew from school—they believed in a bond of faith with the West and, implicitly, a common enemy in Islam.

But my answers never satisfied them. I quickly learned that saying that I was "culturally Christian," or "agnostic" was pointless—the concepts simply did not exist. A demure "I'm Christian," with lowered eyes, was enough for a few, but many Muslims pressed on.

"But Christianity doesn't make sense. A god who has a son, who is a man, who is also a white bird? How can you believe that?"

"I agree, that doesn't make sense. I don't believe that."

"So you're not a Christian after all," triumphantly. "Do you go to church?"

"Well, not often."

"So you're an atheist!" This was a trap to be avoided at all costs. Atheism was regarded with as much horror as a deadly epidemic disease and thought to be equally contagious. I had heard otherwise reasonable people argue that atheists should be killed, or at least face solitary life imprisonment, to stop them spreading their beliefs.

"Not really, I do believe there is something higher than ourselves . . ."

"So what is this something?" sarcastically. "What rules does it want you to obey? I feel sorry for you Westerners—you don't even know what you believe."

I didn't like my questioners' scornful expressions, and their easy assumption of moral superiority irritated me. It puzzled me too, because a generation previously, middle-class society had been far less ostentatiously devout. The socialist Nasser years had succeeded in pushing Islam to the side of life for affluent Egyptians. Although outright atheism was still reviled, for many observance dwindled to a laissez-faire celebration of the big holidays, weddings and funerals, occasional prayers and social events at the mosque. As they were growing up in the 1980s and '90s, my Egyptian contemporaries were taught to fear "Islamist terrorists" as much as to resent "Zionist oppressors."

Now piety was sweeping the middle classes again. Everyone was talking about a trendy young preacher called Amr Khaled, so popular he'd been kicked out of the country by the government and was biding his time in my home city of London.[2] Gradually, I met more and more educated young people who were turning to conservative religion as a way of creating meaning in their lives, joining a community with a shared purpose and—as my conversations showed—proudly asserting their difference from the West. What surprised me was that it was often an act of defiance against their parents' generation and the unjust, corrupt society they had helped create. It seemed paradoxical to me—I expected rebellion to always be about the desire for what I perceived as freedom. But for some the restrictions of conservative religion were proving a liberation. I wanted to find out more about what was inspiring them.

It was hard to imagine a more unlikely recruit to the Salafis' message of asceticism and hellfire than Ayman. He had grown up with his parents and younger brother in a spacious Cairo suburb, his life a relaxed, predictable round of school—an English-language private college that boasted it had educated King Farouk, the last king of Egypt—football practice, American movies and summer trips to the beaches of the Mediterranean coast. His mother wanted him to become an engineer, his father, a police officer.

In September 2000, as his parents watched the television news, he had seen a Gazan boy called Muhammad al-Durrah killed in crossfire between Israeli soldiers and Palestinian security forces. Muhammad was twelve, exactly the same age as Ayman. The footage of him screaming in terror, huddling behind his father, was repeated on loop.[3] Ayman was transfixed, tears streaming down his face. As he wiped them, he remembered a film he had just seen about a blue-collar student who enrolled at the snobbiest university in Cairo. In one scene, the hero had burned an Israeli flag in front of his sissy, Westernized classmates.

Ayman had no idea where he could find an Israeli flag, so he carefully drew its blue bands and six-pointed star on a big sheet of paper and stole a box of matches from his mother's kitchen. When he arrived at school the next day, he marched straight to the front of the classroom, unfurled his homemade flag and set it ablaze. His classmates began to clap, cheering and shouting, and teachers gathered in the doorway as the flames licked up the paper. Ayman, flushed and elated, saw that some of them were applauding too. The headmistress called his parents to school, and Ayman thought that he would be punished. But they discovered that boys in other grades had copied him and burned Israeli flags in their classrooms. Teachers queued up to shake his father's hand, saying, "Congratulations sir, you should be very proud of Ayman."

Ayman's parents weren't so sure. They lived by the motto "walk next to the wall"—keep a low profile and avoid politics. The family had been in official favor for years. Ayman's father made famous sculptures in the nationalist style, towering granite figures that held the Nile protectively in their hands or stood guard over the beloved homeland. In the 1980s the state had invited him to decorate a huge North Korean–funded panorama celebrating the 1973 war with Israel, and he spent months carving friezes of heroic Egyptian soldiers crossing the Suez Canal to attack the cowering occupiers of the Sinai. Ayman and his brother grew up hearing that Anwar Sadat—who had led the war and secured the peace treaty that eventually returned the Israeli-occupied Sinai to Egypt—was "the hero of war and peace."

Now Ayman started to feel that his father was wrong. Sadat wasn't a hero, and Egyptians should have fought like men and taken back the Sinai without the shameful treaty. For him, as for Amr, the conflict in Palestine was becoming a gateway to thinking about injustice closer to home. When he saw disabled people begging in the street and the poor queueing for rough subsidized bread, the streets strewn with garbage and the broken-down cars and buildings, he realized that Mubarak and his regime were also criminals.

The military regime that his father wanted him to love had created this oppression, and consumerism was just a distraction from it. Perhaps Islam, which distinguished the Arab world from Israel and the West, held an answer. His fashionable school taught only cursory religious lessons, but Ayman secretly began to read and study for himself, looking for answers. As he grew into a teenager his classmates began to come to him, asking simple questions. "How should I fast properly like the Prophet did?" or "Is it forbidden or allowed to smoke cigarettes, wear shorts in the street, disobey my parents?" When he answered them, he felt as proud and certain as when he'd brandished the flaming flag. Inside him, a fierce devotion to the Prophet began to burn. He was the perfect man: the ultimate warrior, judge and ruler. The Prophet, Ayman was certain, would have been able to root out all the corruption in Egypt, and right all of its injustice.

Whatever the Salafis thought, religious fervor was no new phenomenon in Egypt. The country had been Muslim since the Prophet's Companion Amr ibn al-'As had conquered it for the caliphate in 640, and it had developed its own Islamic folk beliefs and traditions. Among them were thousands of *moulids*—festivals held around saints' shrines that mixed music with ecstatic chanting, prayers, fairground rides, sweets, fireworks and communal visits to the shrine—that could draw hundreds of thousands of people. In contrast to Salafi puritanism, these ceremonies were eclectic—they might draw on Christian beliefs, animist traditions brought by slaves and laborers from Sudan and East Africa and even ancient Egyptian rites. The most heterogeneous of them all was the *zar*, a healing ceremony that used drumming and the music of a large resonant lyre called the *tanbura* to cure people possessed by dangerous spirits.

In the twenty-first century the *zar* was a dwindling, secretive practice and I never expected to witness one. But in 2009 a musicologist called Zakaria Ibrahim invited me to visit him in Port Said, the freewheeling port city where the Suez Canal meets the Mediterranean. One April evening, as the sun was sinking into the desert beyond the city, I drove with Zakaria out to a row of scruffy concrete housing blocks to visit Sheikha Zeinab, the last *zar* mistress in Port Said. The front room of her tiny apartment was thick with the smoke of cigarettes, hashish and incense, and packed with heavyset working-class women in brightly colored house gowns. All had come to be treated for psychological problems—depression, anxiety, constant weeping or unexplained phantom pains—they believed were caused by spirits. Three slight, elderly men who squatted along one wall, smoking hashish in water pipes, introduced themselves as the musicians—Bulbul, whose nickname meant Nightingale, Abu Hossein and Araby Jacomo the *tanbura* master. They let Zakaria attend the *zar*, which was closed to outsiders, because to gain their trust he had spent a year serving them, carrying the incense at ceremonies and collecting their fees from patients.

The ceremony began in darkness, lit only by an altar bearing two candles and a shallow bowl of unshelled peanuts, toffees and dry beans. Sheikha Zeinab, a round-faced woman in her sixties wrapped in the black gown and headscarf traditionally worn by older women, circled the room with a plate of incense smoldering on charcoal, dousing us all in smoke. Then Bulbul struck up a rapid, skittering drumbeat. Three of the women, long white cloths draped over their heads and faces, threw themselves into the center of the room and began to dance. Led by Sheikha Zeinab, the musicians spurred them on through call-and-response songs, clattering cymbals, handclaps and drums, all underpinned by the soft, dry tones of the *tanbura*. In the tiny space, the sound was overwhelming. As I watched from my seat on the floor, the women collapsed on all fours or threw themselves full-length to the ground wailing and crying, then staggered to their feet as Sheikha Zeinab exhorted the spirits to have mercy on them. After two hours, the music slowed, then stopped. Exhausted, the musicians and patients sat together in the light of the candles, sharing the toffees from the altar.

I went over to sit by Sheikha Zeinab and Bulbul, a small, mischievous-looking man who said he had been playing at *zars* for fifty years. He explained that people could be possessed by Muslim, Christian, male, female or child spirits, whose names and characteristics reflected *zar*'s roots in Egypt and Sudan.

"Who are the spirits?" I asked.

"There are so many, but there are three who are most important," he said. "Yawra Bey, who is the king of the Muslim spirits. He's a dandy, dressed in that long black coat like the Europeans used to wear—what is it called?"

"A frock coat?"

"Yes, that—and he carries a sword. Then there is Lady Racosha, who is a naughty girl child spirit. Then the Red Djinn, who is the leader of the Christian spirits."

I turned to Sheikha Zeinab, who was still breathing heavily from her hours of singing and dancing. "How can you tell the difference between these spirits, Sheikha?"

"One way is that they ask me for different things, as payment for leaving the patients alone," she said, drawing deeply on her cigarette. "Christian spirits usually demand bananas, apples, beer or whisky; Muslim spirits want peanuts or beans, like we have on the altar there." She was holding the hand of one of the patients who sat by her, leaning against the wall with her eyes closed, utterly drained. I smiled at her, liking her compassion. I could see her *zar* ceremony gave women living harsh lives in traditional communities a space of freedom where they could blame forbidden acts like smoking cigarettes or hashish, drinking and even screaming and crying on the control of the spirits, and find support for problems that they had no other way to discuss.

"Why is *zar* dying out?" I asked.

"The Salafis. The religious fanatics," Sheikha Zeinab said simply. "These religious TV channels that broadcast from Saudi Arabia are telling people that *zar* is un-Islamic and wrong. If they have a problem, they should call the channels' own religious experts—on a premium-rate phone line, of course—about it instead."

"The bearded ones interrupt us now," said Bulbul. "They scream at the patients, and force us to stop playing. People are scared to ask us to perform a *zar* for them, and when we do we have to hide."

The *zar*, with its wild space of liberation, drinking, smoking, music, dancing and mixing of men and women, was anathema to the Salafis' vision of a single globalized, uniform faith. But even averagely devout young Egyptians had no time for folk religion. It was backward-looking and embarrassingly local when they wanted to be modern and global. "Official" religion had little to offer them. Al-Azhar, the grand mosque and university that had been Egypt's highest Islamic authority for one thousand years, had been co-opted by the state, its government-vetted officials offering bland ritual safely isolated from politics. There was no one to preach modern Islam to a generation raised on Hollywood movies, computer games and music videos.

Ahmed Abu Haiba knew he was the man to change that. A TV magnate with sharp eyes, a quick brain and the bull-necked build of a boxer, he looked at Egypt's neglected, frustrated young people and saw not the burden that the government did, but an opportunity. Whoever could tap into the energy and enthusiasm that was burning itself out in Cairo's suburbs or run-down provincial towns, he realized, would control Egypt's future.

He had been recruited by the Muslim Brotherhood as a teenager in the 1980s. At meetings, he met a boy of the same age called Amr Khaled, with a hypnotic gentle voice and a gift for persuasion. In the Brotherhood's training system of "family" groups, they were schooled in the belief that Islam could never be simply a private faith that need not impinge on public life. That was a distortion of its message peddled by the West and the corrupt local regimes it propped up. "Islam," the Brotherhood's founder Hassan al-Banna had written, "is a comprehensive system which deals with all spheres of life." It stretched from politics to justice, culture to business, warfare to, finally, worship.

This belief arose out of the time of the Brotherhood's founding, as the Ottoman Empire—believed by some to be the last remnant of the original Islamic caliphate—crumbled and the Middle East fell further under Western control. The key to reversing the rise of the West, the Brothers believed, was *da'wa*—the "call" to spread Islam as it should be observed, Brotherhood-style. It wasn't only the duty of religious scholars, but of every Muslim. And just as Islam provided guidance for all spheres of life, anything it permitted—sports, entertainment, business, even personal relationships—could be used to spread the true faith.

By his early thirties, Abu Haiba was working in television, but he was still devoted to *da'wa*. His talent was to take inspiration from hit American TV shows, and produce his own versions carefully tailored to the Middle East. He looked at the megastar American televangelists who commanded audiences of millions, their simple, direct language, their personal stories, their extravagant emotions, their glitzy presentation, and thought—*I could do the same thing for Islam.*

He found the perfect star in his old friend Amr Khaled, who had quit his job as an accountant to preach to Cairo's rich and famous. In 1999, the two young men put together an Islamic TV series called *Words from the Heart*. The name was significant. Instead of thundering about hellfire, Amr Khaled rhapsodized about God's love. He wore jeans and shirts instead of robes and spoke not classical Arabic but the same informal Egyptian dialect as his listeners. He chatted about football, family, holidays, studying and friendship— mixing personal testimonies, simple stories about the lives of the Prophet and his Companions, tears and laughter. Amr

Khaled's style was inclusive—he wasn't openly aligned with the Brotherhood, and neither did he discuss politics. Young people, directionless and stifled, flocked to him; his cassettes and videos sold in their hundreds of thousands. The audience at his Friday sermons in the upmarket district of Dokki spilled into the streets outside the mosque. His mobile rang constantly with young fans seeking spiritual guidance.

Like the American evangelical preachers with their tales of being "born again," Amr Khaled emphasized spiritual transformation—starting with his own tale of abandoning his promising accountancy career for a life devoted to God. If he could rediscover his faith, he said, so could his audience. And for women, that meant putting on the headscarf and the conservative clothing that accompanied it. In a taped sermon that swept Egypt, Amr Khaled spoke emotionally about the "greatest thing that belongs to women":

> When the enemy of Islam wants to attack something, the first thing they attack is the woman! Because when the woman loses her modesty, it is easy for the man to be lost, and it is in turn easy for the whole society to lose its modesty . . . And the most important thing for the woman, the greatest thing for her. What is it? For her to protect and cover her body. The greatest thing that belongs to the woman is her hijab.[4]

In the 1960s and '70s, Egyptian films had been the most famous in the Middle East, their glamorous female stars clad in Western-style sundresses and swimsuits. Now, one after another, actresses began to "retire," putting on the headscarf and denouncing their former profession as immodest and ungodly. Abu Haiba, knowing repentant sinners made great TV, coaxed them back into the spotlight to share dramatic stories: one had been inspired to wear the headscarf after attending a life-changing lecture by Amr Khaled; a second after the dance music she was listening to was mysteriously replaced by Quranic recitation; a third after a dream in which God stretched out his hands to her.

Thousands, then tens of thousands, then hundreds of thousands of ordinary Egyptian women imitated them. While women in villages like Amal's had re-adopted the headscarf years earlier, it was now spreading to the urban middle and upper classes. An urban legend circulated that Amr Khaled had convinced Hosni Mubarak's daughter-in-law to wear the veil, embarrassing the unveiled First Lady, Suzanne Mubarak.

It was a belated revenge for the Brotherhood. In 1966, Nasser had given a speech recalling a meeting with the head of the movement, Hassan el-Hodaiby, in 1953, soon after the Brotherhood had helped bring him to power.

"The first thing he asked for," said the president, "was to make wearing the hijab mandatory in Egypt, and demand that every woman walking in the street should wear a headscarf."

He paused, wryly, and his audience sniggered.

"Let him wear it!" heckled one.

Nasser grinned, cruelly.[5] By that time, el-Hodaiby was locked in one of Nasser's jails, the Brotherhood was banned and its desire for a visibly Islamic society seemed like a distant memory. But forty years later it was old photos and movies showing middle-class women swimming, sunbathing and picnicking in Western-style clothes that looked shocking. Cairo's streets were more outwardly pious than they had been for a century.

The state portrayed Islamists as poor and backward, rabid bigots bent on destroying modern society. But Amr Khaled was rich, educated and charming. Religious fervor was sweeping exclusive sports clubs, top universities and Cairo's most desirable addresses. Amr Khaled condemned all kinds of violence and extremism. But his growing popularity among young Egyptians made the state nervous, and the authorities moved in.

State security told Amr Khaled he would have to stop preaching unless he moved to a mosque in 6th of October City, a windswept satellite city that downtown Cairenes considered the end of the earth. Amr Khaled obediently moved. After a few weeks, the spies were stunned. On Friday mornings coaches, minibuses and cars blocked the highways of 6th of October City as far as the eye could see. Thousands, then tens of thousands of young people poured out of them to hear their hero speak. He didn't call for the overthrow of the government, or criticize the Mubaraks by name, but eventually the regime had had enough. In 2002, Amr Khaled was forced to leave for London. His public preaching career had lasted just three years.

If the authorities thought that exiling Amr Khaled would curb young Egyptians' fascination with religion, they were to be disappointed. Encouraged by his growing status as the class authority on faith, in 2003 fifteen-year-old Ayman bought a tape of Islamic lectures from a street stall. The preacher turned out to be a blind sheikh called Abdel Hamid Kishk, famous for his stentorian voice, sense of humor and ferocious opposition to Nasser, Sadat and Mubarak. On the tape, Kishk was talking about Omar ibn al-Khattab, the second caliph of the Islamic empire, the most just and heroic ruler who had ever followed in the Prophet's footsteps. By way of contrast, Kishk held up the cruel tyrant Hosni Mubarak. Ayman was enraptured. It was the first time he had heard anyone dare criticize the president so bluntly.

"What's that you're listening to?" asked Ayman's father, banging on his bedroom door. He had recently sculpted a frieze of Mubarak offering the gift of nuclear energy to a beautiful woman representing Egypt. "It sounds like that terrible man Abdel Hamid Kishk."

"It is Abdel Hamid Kishk," Ayman told him defiantly. After that, he bought as many tapes as he could afford. He discovered Amr Khaled, whose style was friendly and sympathetic. Ayman convinced his school friend Sherif to listen with him, and soon Sherif was buying tapes and swapping them with Ayman. They began listening to Quranic recitation together, talking about Amr Khaled's lectures, and sitting in the mosque all evening from the dusk prayer until the night prayer, spurred on by their parents' horror at their new piety.

But Amr Khaled's upbeat approach didn't fit with Ayman's anger and frustration. He quickly tired of hearing about relentless positivity, obedience to your parents, love for your fellow citizens, service to your community, hard work, aspiration and achievement. Then he discovered a Salafi preacher called Mohamed Hassan, who sported a badger-striped beard and held forth in fiery, eloquent classical Arabic. Where Amr Khaled's teachings were feel-good, Mohamed Hassan's were fierce, his Islamic references more complex, his judgments harsher but, Ayman felt, more righteous because of that. He discovered other Salafi sheikhs and fell in love with their puritanical worldview, the simplicity of the line they drew between right and wrong, pure and impure.

Though Salafis were closely monitored by state security, they were allowed to gather in mosques, one of which welcomed

Ayman. He began attending five times a day, slipping silently out of the house in the dark for the dawn prayer.

Gradually his opinions became more extreme. As his new friends taught him, he began to believe that Egyptian society was hypocritical, that ordinary people who claimed to be Muslims weren't really Muslims. He began to hate Amr Khaled, whom he had once loved, but now thought was diluting the true message of Islam. He began to hate the Muslim Brotherhood, who were too moderate in their interpretation of the faith. He began to despise the West, the ultimate source of all corruption. The preachers he followed criticized all non-Salafis for being corrupt and impure, and Ayman believed they were right.

It was a lonely existence. Sherif hadn't followed him into Salafism, and Ayman's parents became more and more anxious about his transformation. They called Salafis "the beardy ones," after the luxuriant facial hair they grew, with a mixture of fear and dislike. When they stopped him from going to the mosque, he sat alone in his room listening to *anasheed*, the hypnotic, a capella male-voice religious chants that for Salafis took the place of music. After a string of bombings in Cairo and tourist resorts in 2004 and 2005, Ayman's parents became fearful that their son had been brainwashed and would turn to terrorism or be abducted by state security. They raided his room and confiscated his Salafi tapes and books. Ayman wasn't worried. On one of his tapes, Abdel Hamid Kishk even joked about it. "Oh God, please bless everyone in the second and third rows of the congregation," he said. "What about the first row?" asked a listener. "They're all state security," replied the sheikh.

Ayman was far more concerned about a Hadith that he had heard quoted on his tapes: "Those who make images will be punished on the Day of Judgment and it will be said to them—breathe life into what you have created."[6]

He turned the problem over in his mind, studying books of religious commentary and discovering that "images" included the sculptures and friezes that his father made. Eventually, he called a respected Salafi scholar whose mobile number was passed between acolytes, and asked him for a fatwa, an Islamic legal opinion.

"What should I do, sheikh?" he asked. "I'm still at school, but I'm living in my father's house, and he's a sculptor. Does that mean all his money and everything that comes from it is *haram* forbidden by Islam? How can I be safe?"

"Yes, it is definitely *haram*," the sheikh told him. "I won't tell you you have to leave home now, because you're still at school, but you must only eat and drink just enough to keep yourself alive. Anything more, and you are profiting from unholy work."

Ayman took the advice to heart. Obedience to such a revered scholar, who had studied God's word for so many years, was far more important than obedience to his misguided parents. For the next months, he pushed his food around his plate, and drank only sips of water.

To take his mind off his growling stomach, he sat in his room, reading a famous Salafi scholar's memoirs describing how he had had to leave Egypt and go to Saudi Arabia, the home of Islam and the Prophet, to purify himself. Ayman didn't know what Saudi Arabia was like, but it had to be better than degenerate Egypt, where Mubarak's godless regime seemed certain to endure forever. He would never be a good Muslim, he realized, until he went there, away from everything he knew. He refused to leave first his house, then his room. He felt guilty all the time, because he couldn't live up to the impossible Salafi standard of purity. He sometimes weakened and watched a movie, and he wasn't strong enough to leave his family and flee alone to Saudi Arabia, seeking spiritual salvation. Salafism had led him only to despair.

The hopelessness that gripped Ayman affected many other young Egyptians. They quickly learned that any personal effort could be swept aside in a moment by a galaxy of forces from corruption to bureaucracy, dysfunctional infrastructure or the malevolence of state security. Now, Amr Khaled was offering them a solution. Though the Egyptian government had banned him from preaching, satellite TV made their attempts to silence him irrelevant. In 2004, a Gulf-owned channel aired the first episode of his new show *Life Makers*.

"This is not a television program, it's a project to revitalize our countries and save our youth," Amr Khaled told his viewers. Each week, he set them a new goal—anything from listing their life ambitions, to collecting used clothing for the poor, to treating family members with extra kindness. *Life Makers* was carefully designed to make young people its stars. Viewers' messages were read out onscreen and participants were invited to meet Amr Khaled and share their stories in each episode.

While Ayman was listening to his Salafi sermons, across town in the elegant neighborhood of Heliopolis a curly-haired sixteen-year-old boy called Mazen was watching *Life Makers* with his mother. Mazen went to a private German-language school in Cairo and his father had decreed he would eventually train as a dentist, with the possibility of going into the family petrol business. This combination, his family thought, covered all the bases of respectability, stability and moneymaking potential.

The only problem was that Mazen wasn't interested in any of it. He didn't care about teeth, or petrol, or business, and he rarely saw his father, who spent most of his time in Saudi Arabia with his second wife and family. Mazen was kind and sensitive and what he really loved was animals. Egyptians, with so many poor and uneducated themselves, treated animals brutally. Cairo was full of skeletal, sore-covered working donkeys and horses, and feral cats and dogs that adults deliberately ran over or poisoned, and children kicked and tortured. Mazen and his mother took the dogs and cats in, vaccinated them and fed them until they recovered. But veterinary work was no career for the son of a successful businessman.

Then Mazen heard about *Life Makers*. He carried out the weekly tasks as earnestly as if Amr Khaled himself was supervising him, making lists of his personal goals and posting them off to the channel, saving his pocket money to print out surveys at an Internet cafe and taking them to school.

"What do you think are the main challenges facing Egyptian society?" he asked his friends and teachers, and dutifully recorded all their answers. By the end of the day, he had collected a sheaf of surveys he could send off to *Life Makers*, and he felt proud. Then a secretary caught him and sent him to the headmaster.

"What's all this?" the headmaster asked Mazen, waving at his stack of papers.

"It's a survey about our country, from *Life Makers*," Mazen replied eagerly. "Please will you fill one in, sir?"

The principal looked at him, less angry than anxious. "Oh no, we can't have things like that in school," he said. "It might make trouble, and we don't want that here." Like everyone else, he was afraid of the security services.

It was this timid mindset that Amr Khaled was trying to eradicate. His vision of a self-reliant, entrepreneurial new generation had much in common with his opponent Gamal Mubarak's. In the eyes of the Life Makers youth group and projects inspired by the TV show, nothing would ever come of waiting for the state to fix the broken education and health-care systems, the faltering economy and lack of innovation and opportunity. Young people were no longer doomed to be either passive beneficiaries of the state, as they might have seen themselves under Nasser, or passive victims of its failures, as they might see themselves under Mubarak. It was up to them to solve these problems themselves. And in doing so, Amr Khaled promised, they would discover a new sense of power and purpose.

"Change starts with yourself," he told his viewers as Mazen took notes in an old schoolbook, exhorting them not to smoke, to take regular exercise, to study hard, to learn about goal-setting, time management and performance reviews. These ideas, Amr Khaled admitted, borrowed heavily from American self-improvement books like Stephen R. Covey's *The 7 Habits of Highly Effective People*—though he said all the advice he found in such books was already contained in the Quran and Hadiths.[7]

By the time the TV series ended in 2005, it had left a growing network of Life Makers youth groups across Egypt, Jordan, Palestine, Yemen, Morocco, the UK and beyond. Amr Khaled himself had inspired a crop of handsome young televangelists who became known as "the new preachers." They wore jeans and trainers and slipped easily from Arabic to English; from TV studios in Dubai to speaking tours of the UK; from Quranic quotations and stories of the Prophet to anecdotes about the present almost as if there was no time between the seventh century and the twenty-first. It was a globalized faith that mirrored the disjointed modern environment inhabited by middle-class Egyptians like Ayman and Mazen—newly built housing compounds, air-conditioned chain cafes, shopping malls, highways and the Internet.[8]

Ahmed Abu Haiba, who had created Amr Khaled's first show, was still at the forefront of this "new Islam." To win over media-savvy twenty-first-century youngsters, he was convinced he needed an irresistible blend of Western media and Islamic message. For the last decade, young Egyptians had been hooked on the local music channels that showed nonstop videos of the biggest Arab stars, lavishly muscled hunks and unveiled, heavily made-up women in miniskirts and skintight dresses. Abu Haiba played a group of Saudi investors a montage of the raunchiest of the videos. One featured a minidress-clad Lebanese singer gyrating while pouting, "At your service, sir." Horrified by what they saw, the investors begged him to turn it off.

"*This* is what your children are watching on television," Abu Haiba told them. Immediately, they agreed to find the cash for a "clean" alternative.[9]

In 2009, Abu Haiba launched Islam's answer to MTV—4Shbab, "For Youth." 4Shbab featured good-looking pop stars from Syria, Saudi Arabia, Yemen and Egypt—and no women at all. Its music videos, chat shows and talent contests were snappy, fun and colorful, but they exhorted viewers to "listen to the tune of Islam."

Soon afterward, I went to watch his team shoot their latest music video—a story about a devout student going to study in the West, successfully resisting temptation and returning more pious than ever and with an international corporate job—in a five-star hotel in the desert outside Cairo.

When the crew took a break I sat down next to the director amid a rubble of Diet Pepsi cans and crumpled cigarette packets. Slim, black-clad and heavily stubbled, Nour looked like any auteur from Paris or Berlin. He had made videos for the Arab world's bare-chested pop hunks and gyrating pop starlets before Ahmed recruited him to create the same slick look—plus shirts and minus any women at all—for the new channel. "I did it all," Nour said to me, tapping ash from a Marlboro Light. "I worked with all the big names, made videos about love and beautiful women. But I became bored. Now I'm finally making a video about a relationship with a real meaning—the one between man and God."

Nour went back to check his monitors, and I stood in the chilly marble-floored corridor with the star. Rabea Hafiz was a twenty-seven-year-old singer who had spent his life training in classical Quranic recitation. He was handsome in an otherworldly way, with deep brown eyes behind rimless glasses and a shy smile—but his heart was set on pop success. Abu Haiba's plan was to create a new range of celebrities to fit his new medium, and Rabea had been talent-scouted for his clean-cut look and religious credentials.

"With 4Shbab I know I'm making something clean," he said as we drank tea out of disposable cups. "It's not one of those dirty music videos." He sounded like he was reassuring himself. The *Story of Success* shoot was Rabea's first for the channel and the first time he had met Abu Haiba. He shifted foot to foot apprehensively when the boss strode along the corridor toward us. I understood his nerves. Abu Haiba had an uncompromising commitment to high standards in both faith and showbiz.

"We need more handsome stars like this one, with a good commercial mentality," Abu Haiba observed to me when he reached us. He looked Rabea over briskly, confiscated his glasses and coaxed his dark hair into a more telegenic wave. "OK, let's hear the famous voice," he ordered. Rabea shyly opened his mouth to sing and was transformed, smiling slightly as the beautiful plaintive sound echoed through the hotel corridor. Abu Haiba nodded in satisfaction and strode off. They were hoping Rabea would join the handful of global Islamic music megastars—English-language singers such as the Swedish–Lebanese Maher Zain, who filled stadiums from the United States to Malaysia, from South Africa to Turkey. Islamic pop was becoming big international business. Stars like Zain offered their fans a precious commodity—the ability to draw meaning and hope from everyday frustrations. They also offered licit eye-candy for Muslim girls uneasy about devoting themselves to their direct competitors— Justin Bieber or One Direction.

Salafis and other conservative Muslims were horrified by Abu Haiba's tactic of turning Western entertainment to the service of Islam. Shortly after my visit to the video shoot, I saw Abu Haiba in a TV debate with a conservative scholar.

"This whole idea is American Islam," thundered the white-bearded octogenarian scholar. "You know what your channel is saying? That the Holy Quran is impotent, that it cannot reach youth. That our religion is useless. Islam already has its modes of communication. Those who don't follow us can go to hell."

Abu Haiba shrugged. "Cars are a Western idea," he said. "TV is a Western idea. Does that make everyone who uses them a traitor? All media innovation comes from the West. I see music videos, films, sitcoms, just as vehicles for my Islamic message."

The camera panned back to the scholar, whose eyes bulged. "Has God's word become inferior to music, dance and women?" he demanded.[10]

For the old-fashioned scholar, Western culture was the enemy. For Abu Haiba and Amr Khaled, it was just another tool.

The Life Makers had little in common with the liberal bloggers and leftist activists who were leading small protests on the streets in Cairo. But behind the scenes, their apparently innocuous activities were training thousands of young people in self-reliance and the desire for change.

I met Mazen in 2010, at a youth volunteering evening in Cairo. He had graduated in dentistry now, and was working part-time in a dental clinic near his home. Practice had given him no more love of his profession than before.

"Why would I want to look inside people's smelly mouths?" he asked in outrage. "Teeth are disgusting."

I was quite glad Mazen wasn't working full-time. He told gruesome stories of dentistry students botching anaesthetic injections, knocking out the poor patients who came to the student clinic. Instead, he filled his time studying Islam and volunteering. He was an inveterate volunteer—distributing food, teaching English, bringing clean running water to poor villages. When he talked about the projects, he lit up with pride and optimism.

He belonged to a branch of Life Makers in northern Cairo that ran development and charity projects from used-clothing drives to literacy classes. That summer of 2010 he took me to meet them in the language-school classroom where they met after hours amid stacks of chairs and tables.

It was a bleak time to be young in Egypt, with daily struggles with fraying infrastructure, bureaucracy, corruption and unemployment. But the Life Makers crackled with energy. They were all in their late teens and twenties—student doctors, engineers and accountants—and though they were volunteers they had given their group all the trappings of the corporate world. They had a CEO and VPs, PowerPoint presentations, project reports, training manuals and mission statements. The sense of purpose and determination in the room was tangible, and the way they talked would have made worrying listening for the state.

The state had tried to teach these young people that Islamists were evil. It expected them to accept oppression, surveillance and lack of opportunity. It showed them that the only way to succeed was through corruption and nepotism— Gamal Mubarak being living proof. It wanted compliance as the price of their safety. This bargain had worked, more or less, for their parents' generation, who had been lifted out of rural poverty, given modern tertiary education and modern housing in the cities, and steady jobs in the bureaucracy with perks and pensions. To inspire them, they'd had first Nasser's dream of a pan-Arab Middle East led by Egypt, then Sadat's get-rich-quick promises of Western-style wealth. But as Mubarak's rule wore on, the state had less and less to offer young people like Mazen. It was economically weak and ideologically bankrupt.

Now, Islam had given them a solid foundation of certainty. It answered existential questions; it gave meaning to petty everyday frustrations and dilemmas; and it bracketed all unanswerables into the category "God knows better than us." Life Makers had taught them that they didn't have to bow to the state, its police or its army. These man-made constructs were insignificant before the almighty power of God.

Rehab, a demurely dressed girl with a sweet, serious expression, took my hand. The force of her words, coming from her tiny frame, was disconcerting.

"We're learning that if we organize and reach a critical mass, we can make a change," she said. "Allah promises that good people will prevail and achieve what they are aspiring to. Without what we've learned from Life Makers, we would have given up long ago."

Her friend Ahmed agreed. He was a skinny young man with a prematurely receding hairline and a big smile, who had led a project to distribute Ramadan food packages to poor families.

" 'The government' is the big ghost, the big illusory monster for us," he told me. I was surprised to hear an ordinary person criticize the regime so directly. "It always made us feel like we can't do anything. But with this project, we tried to do something and we achieved it. I can't describe the smiles and the happiness of the people we helped. I didn't need the government to help me with any of it, and they couldn't stop me either."

In Mubarak's Egypt it was easy, as Ayman's story showed, for even the most educated and Westernized young Egyptians to be drawn to hard-line Islam. Salafism offered black-and-white answers amid the chaos of life in a dysfunctional dictatorship; and the chance to be pure and righteous when more material forms of achievement were out of reach. And by cultivating the Salafis as a counterweight to the Muslim Brothers, the regime had helped create a groundswell of social conservatism that was feeding Egyptians' opposition to their rulers. Relying on their avoidance of politics was a risky gamble—the millions listening daily to Salafi sheikhs inveigh against unveiled women and the influence of the West would be easily led by any religious authority who cared to rally them against the corrupt regime.

Ahmed Abu Haiba and Amr Khaled's approach to Islam seemed harmless beside the Salafis' threats of brimstone and eternal torment. This was faith expressed in a way that was as fun and accessible as any Hollywood movie, as uplifting as any Western pop music. But it posed an even greater threat to the regime. For Mazen and his friends, *Life Makers* had given them hope and the inspiration to take action for themselves. As Ahmed told me, it was helping to liberate them from the fear of the state and its police. For the Life Makers, it was now God who was handing out the rewards and punishments, not Hosni Mubarak.

PART TWO

4

The Eighteen Days:
The Revolution Begins

MONDAY, JANUARY 24, 2011

Amr had seen the news from Tunisia, where the dictator Zine al-Abidine Ben Ali's twenty-one-year rule had just been swept away by protests, and read the Facebook calls for action in Egypt. But in the five years he'd lived among Cairo's bloggers and activists he'd seen too many protests spring up and fizzle out not to be skeptical. He was certain not much would happen on January 25. Probably, he thought, no one would turn up. At most, a handful of the same activists would get themselves tear-gassed, beaten or arrested, as usual.

Less than a month earlier, he'd been celebrating New Year in his hometown of Alexandria when the city's largest Coptic church was bombed.[1] Twenty-three people were killed and ninety-seven wounded, most of them worshippers. The state alternately blamed "foreign elements," al-Qaeda, Gaza-based Islamists and Mossad-trained Egyptians for the attack, but rumors spread that the interior minister, Habib el-Adly, was himself involved. One of the injured was a Christian university friend of Amr's, whose wife and toddler daughter had been killed instantly. Amr and another Muslim classmate tried to visit him in the state hospital where he lay, severely burned, under police guard.

"Welcome," his mother told them formally, not meeting their eyes. Amr could see in her face that she blamed all Muslims for her loss.

When they left, Amr's classmate rolled his eyes in disgust. "Did you see how cold she was with us? These Christians are impossible to deal with!"

Amr felt like the earth was giving way under his feet. With ordinary Egyptians turning on each other, he saw no future for the country at all.

Now, listening to his Christian colleagues talk about the protest, he thought with a lurch of surprise that he might be wrong. Amr had always considered Copts politically passive— fearful of Islamists, obedient to their pope, conciliatory toward the regime. Today, they were bolder than he'd ever seen them.

"We'll go out and demonstrate tomorrow," they were saying. "This time it's different, something is really going to happen. Especially if people go in large numbers."

No you won't, thought Amr automatically. But he thought that if even Christians were willing to take to the streets, many people might go out to protest for the first time.

Mazen was sitting in a street cafe in Nasr City, drinking endless glasses of tea to ward off the bone-chilling desert cold and playing poker with his college friends.

"Do you think anything will happen?" the young men asked each other as they hunched deeper into their jackets. They had also seen the sites calling for protest: We Are All Khaled Said, where 300,000 people had said they would participate in the demonstration; the new citizen journalism network Rassd; a video made by an ex–police officer who'd written a book called

How to Avoid Being Hit Over the Head—a guide for civilians in how to deal with the police—then fled to America.

Their friend Mahmoud, a youth member of the Muslim Brotherhood, dropped in to say good-bye. The Brotherhood had officially stated it would not take part in the protests, but Mahmoud had been told by his superiors that he and other youth members would be on the streets tomorrow.

"Are you really going to do it, Mahmoud?" people were asking as they slapped him on the back.

"Nothing will happen," others were saying. "Egyptians are cowards, they won't do anything."

TUESDAY, JANUARY 25

International clients awaiting delivery of IT projects didn't care that the Egyptian government wanted to celebrate its police force or that Egyptians wanted to protest against them, so Amr went to the office as usual. After work, he sat watching the TV coverage of the protests. For months, he'd been looking forward to a rare break, a desert camping trip due to start the next morning. He still didn't think that the protests would be significant enough to cancel it.

Mazen fell asleep at dawn and woke just before the noon prayer. Online, he saw a livestream of crowds pouring through Cairo's streets. They were shouting *"Enzel, enzel!"* "Come down, come down!" beckoning to the people watching, agog, from their balconies to join them. He had never seen anything like it. He fumbled for his mobile and called his cousin.

"We have to join them!" he said. "We'll never forgive ourselves if we don't."

The young men dressed as the websites advised them, using tactics gleaned from the protests in Tunisia—a big coat, a scarf around the neck for tear gas, and scarves wound around their arms under their coats to protect themselves from baton blows. They bought cans of Pepsi, emptied them out and filled them with vinegar, which they'd read was the best thing to use against tear gas. They didn't know, yet, that the Pepsi itself worked better.

Under the emergency law, protest was strictly illegal, and his uncle and older brother both shouted at them not to go. On the bus, Mazen and his cousin sat separately, in case state security stopped it and found them with their scarves and cans of vinegar. The winter afternoon was short and they arrived in Tahrir Square only ten minutes before the dusk prayer. It was the first protest Mazen had ever seen and he thought the crowds looked small, ringed by rows of riot police. *I never thought I was the kind of guy who'd be in a protest*, he said to himself.

When the call to prayer came, they knelt on the tarmac of the square. The police, living up to their godless reputation, tear-gassed them while they were praying. Mazen, feeling proud to be so prepared, soaked his scarf in vinegar and wrapped it round his nose and mouth. He had seen tear-gas attacks in the movies—people simply tied bandanas over their faces and carried on as normal. He didn't understand what was happening when he found he couldn't breathe or see. Blinded, he ran in weaving arcs through the square, panicking. Around him he could hear people shouting to each other, "Rinse with water!" "Don't rinse with water!" "The vinegar doesn't work!"

But some demonstrators—members of the protest movements Kefaya and April 6, Muslim Brothers, students

and the fanatical football fans that Egyptians call the Ultras—
had faced the riot police before. When Mazen's eyes cleared,
he saw they had captured a shield, a helmet and a baton from
a policeman and were brandishing them as trophies, throwing
them from hand to hand across the square. Now, they were
celebrating their own courage, drumming on lampposts and
chanting an old revolutionary poem:

Real men are real men and cowards are cowards
And us real men are gonna stay in this square!

Between the moments of drama, the square was oddly calm.
When the tear gas dissipated, street vendors filtered in from
their refuge on the Nile corniche a few blocks away, sliding
round corners like cats till they were sure it was safe to sell
newspapers and snacks to the protesters. Some good-looking,
long-haired boys and girls Mazen thought looked like liberals
started playing the guitar and singing. He saw the middle-aged
opposition journalist Ibrahim Eissa walking about, saying
loudly, "Our demands are all written down!" He was acting
like a leader, but it didn't look like anyone was paying attention
to him.

In the lull, Mazen and his cousin went over to speak to the
police conscripts, thin, dark-skinned boys of their own age with
rough country accents. They had no idea how to control a crowd
or police a big urban protest, and they looked scared and angry.

"Do you really like Mubarak?" they asked them. "Do you
like the state this country is in? Do you like being forced to
beat your fellow Egyptians?"

Hearing them, the officers screamed at their men—"Don't
speak to them! Sit down on the ground and await orders!"

The conscripts couldn't reply, but some of them grimaced meaningfully and Mazen knew they were on his side. Mazen thought, *Now they will never hit us or gas us, now we've talked to them.*

But soon after midnight someone gave orders for the police to clear the square and the riot police obediently advanced with their gas and batons. Around Mazen, the protesters scattered in all directions. Forgetting to feel frightened, he thought they looked like cockroaches fleeing an insecticide spray, running into the side-streets off the square, choking on the gas.

When he finally arrived home, all his friends were sharing a video from the day's protests. A young man stood small and defiant in the path of an advancing water-cannon truck, his hands on his hips, looking like he would stop it with his willpower alone. It reminded Mazen of the famous image of a man standing in front of a tank in Tiananmen Square. "*Geda', geda',*" screamed the onlookers on the video. "That's a real man!"[2] The protesters were encouraging other Egyptians to "man up"—to demonstrate their masculine credentials by taking on the regime. But despite the macho rhetoric, women were participating in the demonstrations as equals. Shared between thousands, then tens of thousands of users, the video was helping persuade both men and women that the protests meant something, and that they should join them.

WEDNESDAY, JANUARY 26 – THURSDAY, JANUARY 27

On Wednesday morning, Mazen's friends called, asking him to come out and protest. His eyes still red from the gas, Mazen felt afraid. The official holiday was over and everyone had gone back to work and college until Friday, the first day of the weekend.

"If there aren't many of us, I won't come," he told them. "On Friday there'll be more people. I'll come out then." He ended up joining them anyway, but it wasn't like the previous day. He saw a few people waving banners in the crumbling elegant side-streets of downtown Cairo, and a couple of hundred protesters bunched on the steps of the journalists' syndicate, hemmed in by ranks of riot police. They were chanting in standard Arabic, not Egyptian dialect, "The people want the fall of the regime!" It was the chant from the protests that had brought down the Tunisian president. Now, Mazen realized, the protesters wouldn't be satisfied until Mubarak was gone.

The electric word "*thawra,*" revolution, was spreading online. People had hardly dared hope that they could emulate Tunisia's success, but now it was starting to look possible. They knew that Mubarak, who had been a close friend of the Romanian dictator Nicolae Ceaușescu, executed by the army during an anti-communist revolution in 1989, was terrified of his own military turning on him. "This is the fate of all dictators!" they reminded each other online.

On Thursday Mazen stayed at home, following the news online. The Rassd website said protesters were gathering in Talaat Harb Square, but the police couldn't find them. Then they were in Simon Bolivar Square, then in Abdel Moneim Riad Square, but the police couldn't find them. Afterward, his Brotherhood friends told Mazen that this was a long-planned strategy to tire out the riot police. They would keep protesting in small groups, moving rapidly from place to place, all day every day from January 25 to the big marches they knew would happen on January 28, Friday, the traditional day of protest in the Arab world. *I'm naive,* Mazen started to realize. *I'm just into Life Makers and community work, but these other*

Islamists are politically organized. Amr Khaled, the head of Life Makers who Mazen and his friends had respected and trusted so much, still hadn't said a word in support of the protests. Mazen realized, bitterly, that Amr Khaled was afraid of the regime.

FRIDAY, JANUARY 28

The whole country was braced for "the Friday of Anger," the huge anti-regime protests that were expected, and Mazen's older brother had already forbidden him to leave the house. During the night, the government had cut off Internet services and shut down mobile networks. It showed, Mazen thought, just how out of touch and literal-minded the regime was—if young people were sharing protest material on the Internet and over mobile phones, it thought that the solution was to just pull a plug and cut the entire country off from the world.

Early in the morning, Mazen slipped silently out of his family home and joined a group of young men from Life Makers, heading to the protests. The plan was for protesters to gather at major mosques around Cairo, pray the communal Friday noon prayer, then form marches that would converge on Tahrir.

Like most Cairenes Mazen stuck to familiar areas of the huge city, and it was the first time he'd ever been to the middle-class district of Mohandiseen on the west bank of the Nile. He found the mosque where they were due to gather ringed with riot police. The friends couldn't break through, so at noon they knelt to pray on the street outside, shaking out the rugs they'd brought with them both to pray on and as extra padding against the beatings they expected later.

When the march started, snaking down streets Mazen didn't know, the wealthy people of Mohandiseen came down from their apartments to join them. There were girls with perfect makeup and their hair curled like film stars, carrying perfume against what they imagined was the horrible smell of tear gas. The actor Amr Waked came out and Mazen heard people shouting his name. People were shouting "Come down! Join us!" to spectators on their balconies, and the march kept growing. There were rich people, ordinary people, doormen, street sellers. With the protesters near him, Mazen shouted "*Salmiyya, salmiyya*"—"Peaceful, peaceful." They passed a small knot of riot police, who looked afraid. The officer called to them, "I won't hurt you! Just don't hurt us!"

Half an hour later, the attack started. Mazen and his friends ran to a side-street, upwind of the tear gas, and took shelter behind a kiosk whose owner had fled. He saw people taking bottles of Pepsi, against the gas, from the kiosk's fridges and leaving the money for them on the counter. Then a gas canister arced over their heads into a flat overlooking the street and flames began licking from the windows. Enraged, protesters started to throw rocks at the police. Behind Mazen, an empty police transporter parked in the side-street caught fire and exploded. *It looks just like an action movie*, he thought as he ran from the flames.

The march pressed on, the young men kicking away the tear-gas canisters that kept flying toward them, to the bridge over the Nile that led to Tahrir Square. Mazen's friends were lost, swirled away in the powerful surges of the crowd. Mazen forced his way to the side of the march, next to the railings, so that if anything happened he could jump into the river.

The bridge felt so long that day. The police had begun to use rubber bullets, shooting marchers in the legs. A man rolled up his trousers to show his attackers the wound and shouted, "My father was a martyr of the October 6th war with Israel, and look what you're doing to me."

Then they were face-to-face with the ranks of police on the bridge, looking into each other's eyes. Mazen saw a young conscript, his face twisted with hatred, screaming at the marchers, "You're the losers, we're the winners, you're all going to jail and you'll never get out." He saw a protester talking to a helmeted officer who was holding his hands over the man's ears to protect them from the boom of the tear-gas guns. People were still shouting "Peaceful, peaceful." The hours stood still until the afternoon prayer.

The crowd on the bridge was packed as though they were in the metro at rush hour. Mazen pushed his way back to the side and knelt to pray. When the police opened the water cannon on them as they prayed, at first people laughed and joked—"Thanks guys, now we have water for our ritual ablutions." Then a strange silence fell. The rows of police opened and a water-cannon truck raced straight toward the protesters, trying to scatter them.

Suddenly, Mazen found himself in the front row of the crowd. Time slowed. He thought, *I've seen this in* Medal of Honor, *on the PlayStation—a guy with a rifle, moving his head around to take aim.* His eyes locked with the police marksman's and Mazen realised *He wants to kill me.* He turned and ran and ran.

While he was running, he broke down. He saw a young protester with a rubber bullet in his throat, fighting to breathe, a horrible heaving sound struggling from his open mouth. Mazen stumbled to the ground in horror, picked himself up and ran on, sobbing.

He ran to the end of the bridge and into a side-street on the island of Zamalek. His clothes were soaked from the water cannon and he had no idea where he was. In Nasr City or Heliopolis he could take care of himself, but here he didn't know anyone or anywhere. He sank into a patch of grass, crying hysterically, thinking, *When they come I'll hide in the long grass and they won't even know I'm here.* Suddenly, a foreign journalist with an interpreter was standing over him, wanting to interview him. Mazen held up his hand to show he couldn't speak, tears streaming down his face.

He limped across Zamalek, seeing protesters coming from the poor districts across the river. They didn't have Pepsi or elegant scarves against the gas, but pieces of onion or coal, and dirty rags. He saw riot police resting with their boots off, so exhausted they had lain down in the street. Suddenly, he just wanted to go home.

But on the metro, he thought again. This was a battle, and Islam forbade believers, on pain of hellfire, from fleeing a battlefield. It was time for him to prove himself a real Muslim. At Mubarak, the station below Cairo's central train station, he left the train. Clouds of smoke were billowing along the passageways and squads of teenage protesters were running through the station, calling to male passengers, "If you're a real man, come and join us!" Their masculinity at stake, the commuters followed them sheepishly. Seeing how organized and disciplined the boys were, Mazen recognized them as Muslim Brotherhood.

Outside the station, he saw lines of police trucks retreating, carrying riot police away from the center of the city. People were bombarding them with broken bricks and paving stones that rattled off the sheer metal sides of the trucks. On the other side of the road, a line of tanks was advancing, soldiers waving from their turrets. People were screaming ecstatic greetings to them and throwing them flowers that had appeared out of nowhere. Mazen thought, *The army has come, it's the Tunisian scenario, we're saved.* He knew that without military backing there was no way Mubarak could stay in power. No one found it strange that the army had come to safeguard the people's revolution. Egyptians grew up on heroic stories of the revolution of 1952, when the Free Officers had overthrown King Farouk. Mazen thought, *Now we're victorious, I can go home.*

He started walking toward north Cairo, passing kids playing in the street and shouting, "The police are gone, we kicked them out!" A middle-aged man looked down from his balcony and saw Mazen, soaked from the water cannon, coming home.

"Weren't you afraid?" he shouted admiringly, as if to a hero.

"I didn't have a choice," Mazen replied hoarsely. He had lost his voice from the gas and the crying and the shouting. But he felt proud.

The Internet was still cut, but on the TV, at home, he saw police vehicles burning in Tahrir, the army taking over the state TV and radio building at Maspero, and the hated NDP building, the headquarters of Mubarak's ruling party, ablaze. Then he saw that a second march had come from working-class areas over the bridge where Mazen had run away, and forced its way into Tahrir. Mazen thought, *These guys were like—Forget "peaceful," these sissies from Mohandiseen couldn't do the job!*

Amr and his friends were marooned in the remote Western Desert on their camping trip, following the news as best they could on a radio. They jeered when they heard that King Abdullah of Saudi Arabia had condemned the protests and called Mubarak to express his support. "No Arab and Muslim human being can bear that some infiltrators, in the name of freedom of expression, have infiltrated into the brotherly people of Egypt to destabilize its security and stability," the king had stated. The region's other defenders of the status quo had rallied round the Egyptian president. Mahmoud Abbas, from the Palestinian Authority, had also called Mubarak to "affirm his solidarity with Egypt and his commitment to its security and stability." And the Israelis had called, and been reassured by Mubarak that "this is not Beirut and not Tunis."[3]

Amr's friend Khaled was furious. He was a veteran activist and had attended every protest against Mubarak for the last ten years—except the one that really mattered.

"It's all because of you," he screamed at Amr. "I told you it would be different this time, I've wasted this golden opportunity!"

"Calm down, there will be a lot more fights after this," Amr told him, "and you can attend all of them."

But Khaled wouldn't be comforted. In the middle of the desert he protested by himself, standing on a big rock shouting the chant from Tahrir—"*Irhal!*" "Leave!"

SATURDAY, JANUARY 29

As Amr and his friends drove back into Cairo, they saw the Carrefour hypermarket on its outskirts, a mainstay of middle-class Cairene life, smashed and looted. There was no Internet, no mobile network and no way to reach their friends protesting in Tahrir. There was no sign of the police, and rumors fueled by state media swirled about criminal gangs advancing on middle-class areas. Without Mubarak, they hinted, Egypt would be swallowed by a dark chaos. Everyone was afraid. In each street, the men formed self-defense groups they called people's committees, armed themselves with knives and sticks, and set up checkpoints to stop traffic and defend their homes. The committees were a sign that the regime's power structures were crumbling. The authority that had bounded their existences for as long as they could remember was seemingly vanishing.

Exhausted, Mazen slept. When he woke that evening, there were rumors that "they"—who, was unclear—had opened the jails, that the country's worst criminals were coming to rob and murder people in their homes. For middle-class Egyptians like Mazen's family, who had lived all their lives in a police state where violent crime was almost unknown, it felt like the foundations of their world were crumbling. People were looting and burning the big police station near his home in Nasr City. In the street below Mazen's apartment, residents were banging on lampposts and shouting, "All the men come down!"

Mazen and his brother ran down to join the people's committee. His brother had fashioned a makeshift spear with a knife lashed to a pole and Mazen took it, feeling better once he was armed. They set up a checkpoint and searched all the vehicles that came through, demanding the drivers' IDs. In one truck they found a huge bag of drugs—hashish, pills and powders they couldn't identify. Mazen, who believed Islam forbade all drugs, collected them into a heap and set fire to them. The doormen, who like many Egyptian men felt smoking hashish was practically a human right, stood around the blaze looking sad. Later, Mazen found that some of them had sneaked bits of the hashish and were smoking it in the people's committee while everyone sat around talking about the crisis.

TUESDAY, FEBRUARY 1

Amr, sitting up late in his people's committee, saw that a televised speech Mubarak had made to the nation—appealing to the people's long-held deference for father figures—had split the men around him. The pro-Mubarak men wept with sympathy and shame. How could they have betrayed a man who had devoted his life to the nation?

"I've hated him my whole life, and in five minutes he made me respect him," said a chemistry graduate who made the Molotov cocktails they had stockpiled for protection against criminals, and had protested on January 25.

"Don't listen to this old monster's bullshit, he has to go!" said the dedicated young revolutionaries.

"OK, we might not get rid of him straightaway, but at least we've proven ourselves," said Amr, the pragmatist. Unlike the idealists who believed the entire country had risen up against Mubarak, he thought that most of the 80 million Egyptians were probably against the revolution. It would be reckless to insist that Mubarak step down straight away. Later, he knew that he had been wrong. *If we had believed the promises Mubarak made and let him stay in office*, he thought, *I bet half of my friends would have been hanged from the lampposts.*

Mazen's people's committee was a cross-section of Egypt—Christians, Muslims, regime supporters, revolutionaries, poor people and rich people all united to defend their homes against unknown attackers—and Mubarak's speech divided it, too.

"He's served the country his whole life, what more do you want from him?" Mazen heard people saying as he sat by the watchfire, bundled up against the night cold.

"This madness has to end. There are jihadis in the country, they'll kill us all if we get rid of Mubarak!" a pro-regime businessman was shouting. That was when Mazen broke down again.

"We've got to get a boat, get to Europe, get out of Egypt any way we can," he kept saying. The men thought he was crazy, but he was terrified that the revolution that had barely begun was over, that the army he thought had come to save the people would instead prop up the dictator.

WEDNESDAY, FEBRUARY 2

As the mobile networks were gradually switched back on, Amr started to receive calls from friends protesting in Tahrir, begging *Please join us*. But he remembered the conversation in the people's committee and thought again that the rest of the country was against the revolutionaries and it was madness to continue protesting. He decided it was more urgent to check on his elderly parents in Alexandria.

At Cairo's central station he found the trains weren't running, so he took a microbus the three hours along the desert road to Alexandria. When he reached his parents' home, he got a call from his manager.

"We have a delivery date for this delayed project," he told Amr. "If you have an Internet connection, can you start working on it?"

While he worked, Amr watched the scenes in Tahrir on the TV news. At first, he laughed when he saw men mounted on camels and horses sweeping into the square. It looked too absurd to be dangerous. Then the news worsened. His friends called from Tahrir, asking for help. At 6 p.m. he couldn't take it anymore.

"I have to go back to Cairo," he told his father.

"There's a curfew, they won't even let you into the city. And what about the bandits?" his father protested. There were reports of thousands of escaped prisoners blocking major roads and railway lines, stopping cars and trains to rob people or worse. But Amr found a single microbus willing to make the journey to Cairo. He sat for hours, waiting, until they found fourteen passengers to fill the bus. They traveled silently, in the dark, the driver tense over the wheel. Just before sunrise he threw them out in the west of the city, because he was too afraid to drive anywhere near Tahrir.

On foot, Amr circled through the streets and came toward Tahrir from the east. In a car park five minutes from the square, he saw three tethered horses and seven or eight men bound hand and foot, pro-regime thugs taken prisoner by protesters during the day. He blinked in shock at the scene, which looked like the aftermath of a medieval battle. Mubarak, Amr realized afresh, was a dinosaur. He had switched off the Internet. He had sent camels and horses to do battle in the middle of Cairo. He wanted to drag Egypt back into an unworkable past, ruining the future of a young man like Amr whose career depended on his connections to the twenty-first-century world. From that moment, Amr decided that there would be no more pragmatism and no more compromise. The regime had to go, now.

As the Internet came back on, Mazen found many people online were still supporting Mubarak. He felt too afraid to post anything against the regime. Then he saw a teenage girl sharing revolutionary slogans. Ashamed, he started to share videos of police brutality. The social-media war intensified.

THURSDAY, FEBRUARY 3—THURSDAY, FEBRUARY 10

Every day, now, Amr went to Tahrir with his friends. Ignoring the curfew, they slept in car parks near the square. One night, huddled uncomfortably in a friend's car, the young men began to talk. Before the uprising they had all decided to leave Egypt, because under Mubarak there was no hope for their future. Their applications for immigration as skilled workers to Canada had already been submitted.

"If this thing"—they didn't know what to call the events swirling around them—"turns out to be a real revolution, should we stay or should we still leave?"

"If Mubarak goes, the Islamists will take power."

"It will take another ten years, or more, to get rid of them."

"We don't want to spend the rest of our lives fighting a different kind of authoritarian regime."

Finally, they agreed. "If the people want it, let them taste life under an authoritarian Islamist regime. We will leave."

Mazen stayed at home, looking after his mother and sister and sitting up in the people's committee at night. He thought, *I was in the front lines, I did my job, now let other people do theirs.*

MONDAY, FEBRUARY 7

Amr was working from home, because his company had to keep functioning. He felt that people were getting tired, that the revolution was faltering. But when he saw the TV interview with Wael Ghonim, the Google executive who had set up the We Are All Khaled Said protest on Facebook, he felt things might change. Ghonim had spent the last eleven days in the custody of the security services, blindfolded and cut off from the outside world. When he was released and heard about the protesters who had died, he broke down.

"I'm not a hero," he sobbed. "The real heroes are the ones on the ground."[4]

Amr was happy to know that a software engineer—a man who had harnessed the power of the Internet to bring people together—was one of the icons of this revolution. When he went out to the people's committee that night, he was surprised to find that the sight of the clean-cut young man crying live on TV had shaken the rest of the nation too—even those who didn't know or care about the Internet. People's sympathies began to shift back toward the revolutionaries. Somehow, Wael Ghonim's tears had balanced Mubarak's emotional appeal.

But then, Amr heard rumors of a deal between Omar Suleiman, the feared and hated head of the intelligence services and the new vice president, and the Muslim Brotherhood. People said that Mubarak might go, but that Suleiman would become the next president. Amr thought, *No! We can't let this happen.*

After Wael Ghonim's appearance, the men from Mazen's people's committee also changed their minds. In these fearful, emotional, chaotic times, what they saw on television and heard on the radio could sway their allegiance in moments. Suddenly, each of them resolved to go to Tahrir, to be part of the noble revolution that this brave young man had wept over.

FRIDAY, FEBRUARY 11

Amr decided—*I'm not going to work until Mubarak steps down. It's affecting everything—none of us are safe, the whole country*

125

is breaking down and foreign investors will definitely leave. This last thought was a disaster for a software engineer like Amr— it could destroy his entire future. He went to the protest camp at the parliament building, close to Tahrir. It was full of political activists he hadn't seen since 2007, when he became disillusioned with their endless cycles of protesting, sinking into depression, then protesting again.

Soon after dusk fell, Amr saw a fat man, wearing big headphones, shouting "He's talking, he's talking." Everyone was crowded around him, frozen still, asking what was happening. The fat man started to jump, screaming "He's gone!" Everyone else began to scream too. No one asked what would happen next. A girl jumped into Amr's arms, then she was gone, running. Amr sat on the sidewalk, thinking to himself, *This is too good to be true, there must be a hitch. I need to listen to the speech.* Then he went crazy with joy. He forgot about the immigration application rumbling its way through the Canadian bureaucracy. For the first time in a long time, it felt like Egypt had a future.

When Mubarak stepped down, Mazen was in Tahrir. "*Allahu Akbar!*" the crowds around him shouted, prostrating in thanksgiving. People were dancing around them as they knelt.

"We did it! We killed fear! We're different people now! We'll never be afraid again!" Mazen shouted to his friends. It was the purest joy he had ever felt. He knew they were the generation that had changed Egypt's history, that everything was possible for them, and that nothing would ever be the same.

PART THREE

5

Ayman, Mazen and Abu el-Hassan:
The Battle for Egypt's Soul

In November 2011 I returned to the new Egypt of the revolution. As the sickly orange streetlights and green neon mosque lights of the city rushed up to meet the plane, I remembered a conversation I'd had with Mazen the day after Mubarak stepped down. "We killed fear and laughed in its face," he said, repeating to me what he'd said in Tahrir. "After what I saw and did, I will never be afraid again." I'd never heard anyone speak like that before. Even down the crackly phone line, I could hear the pride and triumph in his voice. Egypt, he was certain, would never be the same.

At the airport it looked like nothing had changed. The bored immigration officers, the police rooting in passengers' luggage for bribes, the scrum of taxi touts, the eternal smell of hot dust, were all the same. Outside, I was hoping to find some of Mazen's ecstatic new sense of possibility.

Instead, I was seeing scenes from the revolution replayed. I rented a cheap room high up in a crumbling colonial building in downtown Cairo, five minutes' walk from Tahrir Square. Off the southeastern corner of the square, in a long high-walled street called Mohamed Mahmoud, young protesters were fighting the security forces. It had started off as a sit-in supporting the families of those killed in the revolution— who everyone called "the martyrs of the eighteen days"—and escalated into a scream of fury against the military council that had taken power when Mubarak stepped down. When the army had arrived in central Cairo on January 28, protesters believed it had come to save the revolution. "*Eid wahda!*" they shouted. "One hand! The army and the people are united." Now, some of them believed, the army was trying to steal it. The protesters also believed that they had proved that the people held the real power in Egypt. They were confident they could defeat the new rulers, just as they'd defeated Mubarak.

I was reporting on the protests for a British magazine, and each day I went down to Tahrir, or circled through the backstreets to approach Mohamed Mahmoud Street indirectly. If the wind was in the right direction, I felt the warning bite of tear gas minutes before I arrived, and heard the distant whipcrack of gunfire. I wasn't afraid of the bullets or the security forces, because as a foreigner I had always— unfairly—felt protected in Egypt. I didn't yet realize that, post-Mubarak, things were changing. Protest was a crash course in its own set of physical skills—run and dodge and throw and jump and duck. I started to understand the tide of adrenaline that kept the protesters going night and day, and to see why most of them were so young. I learned to listen for the rattle of shopkeepers pulling down their metal shutters that signaled a police advance, and for the rhythmic hammering on lampposts and railings the protesters used to drum up their courage before they rushed the security forces' positions.

Mazen's once-glorious Tahrir now looked scruffy and trampled, blocked off to the traffic that usually swirled round its central island. Inside, crowds milled in relative safety, buying tea or makeshift gas masks from the street vendors who followed all the protests, posing for photos in raffishly wrapped keffiyeh scarves, all eyes on the entrance of

Mohamed Mahmoud Street in the corner of the square. They were enjoying the excitement and theater of the protest, but its real menace was in the street itself. That was the territory of the hard-core protesters, the veterans of the eighteen days who knew how to make Molotov cocktails and shelter behind street furniture, the football fans and the kids from rough neighborhoods who hated the police. Through swirling clouds of tear gas, I watched them throwing rocks and Molotovs at the police. They were chanting the most famous chant of the revolution, the one that had jumped like a spark from country to country in the Arab Spring: "The people want the fall of the regime." By way of answer, somewhere in the chaos a police marksman people called "the eye sniper" was blinding protesters with birdshot, one eye at a time. Motorbikes darted through the crowds, ferrying limp bloodstained bodies back from the front lines.

Amal had joined the crowds in Tahrir, and so, separately, had Amr. They both hated the police state. In March, Amr and a group of activists had broken into the looming, fortified state security headquarters in eastern Cairo. The day before, staff had abandoned the compound, driving trucks of hastily shredded files with them. In rooms off the maze of internal courtyards, Amr and his friends found more files, some describing political meetings they'd attended. As they shoveled through the endless records of their state's surveillance of them, other activists came running, laughing and outraged.

"We found the torture cells. And Habib el-Adly's office," they shouted, referring to the hated interior minister who was assumed to have ordered the shooting of protesters and the grotesque attack with horses and camels that Amr had watched from Alexandria. "It has a jacuzzi and his bathrobe is hanging there." For as long as Amr could remember, everyone he knew had been terrified of state security. Now, the cloud of fear they had lived under for decades was dissolving in the bright light of ridicule. High on the adrenaline of Mubarak's departure, they thought the security state was crumbling.

Now, Amr was not so sure. Every so often, canisters came arcing into Tahrir from Mohamed Mahmoud Street, trailing yellow-white plumes of tear gas, and the sounds of gunshots and screams grew louder as the security forces pushed forward to reclaim the square. This was when the festival atmosphere of the square turned sour with real terror, and he ran with the crowds in a panicky stampede past the Egyptian museum and into the side-streets downtown, their walls still crisscrossed with anti-Mubarak graffiti.

Amr had thought, along with the other revolutionaries, that the state's power might have begun to unravel in a more subtle way. The heroes of the revolution were unathletic men like the computer specialists Wael Ghonim and Alaa Abdel Fattah, whose influence came not from physical force or the threat of it, but a newer kind of power. Women had flocked to the streets to demand their rights—not just liberal, unveiled women but conservative women too. They had demonstrated their bravery and ability alongside the men. The alpha male police, who had bullied citizens for so long, had been driven from the streets by their newly empowered victims. Sexual harassment had been virtually unknown for the eighteen days that the protesters had occupied Tahrir Square. And in public, the ruling generals had mouthed pious support of the revolutionaries, "Egypt's glorious youth," and those killed by the security forces, "the martyrs of the eighteen days." As a mark of their sincerity, the metro station that bore the ex-president's name, a busy interchange under Cairo's main rail station, was renamed El-shohada', The Martyrs. Workers went round the metro with black markers, scribbling out the neatly printed "Mubarak" on the carriage maps and scrawling "Martyrs" semi-legibly on top.

But human rights investigations later showed the military had tortured and killed an unknown number of civilians during the revolution, with more than one thousand left missing.[1] *Baltageyya*—plainclothes thugs once hired by Mubarak's regime to maintain deniability—still menaced the streets. Women protesting in the square had been raped and sexually assaulted by gangs. The army itself beat seventeen female protesters and subjected them to forced "virginity tests"—to prevent false allegations of rape, said a general called Abdel Fattah el-Sisi.[2] In the eyes of Egypt's new-old rulers, the revolutionaries were not heroic but decadent: the women promiscuous, "they are not like your daughter or mine," added the general; the men long-haired, effeminate and suspiciously corrupted by Western technologies.

In October, a protest march demanding greater state protection for the Christian minority was attacked by thugs and the military as state TV presenters called on loyal citizens to "defend the soldiers who protected the Egyptian revolution." Twenty-eight protesters were killed, ten of them crushed beneath armored personnel carriers the army drove at speed into the crowds. And in the seven months after Mubarak's overthrow, almost twelve thousand civilians were sent before military tribunals, more than the total during Mubarak's thirty years in power.[3] It was enough to make at least some of "Egypt's glorious youth" doubt their army's love for them.

Mazen was also in Tahrir with his Life Makers friends—the boys darting into Mohamed Mahmoud Street to throw stones and chant against the military council, the girls helping at the field hospitals and blood donation units. On my way to meet him one afternoon, I wove between the street vendors and cut across the square, following two stout middle-aged women whose presence I hoped would give me extra protection from groping hands. Suddenly, the crowds around me panicked at their own tightness and began to surge randomly this way and that, trampling the weakest underfoot, screaming. The women were ripped away from me in a crush that forced the air from my lungs and buckled my knees. Seeing me falling, a young man forced his arms round me, holding me upright and inching enough room for me to breathe. Working patiently with the surges, he dragged me to the margin of the crowd, half-carried me up the street and deposited me at Mazen's feet, bruised but unharmed. "Don't leave her alone again," he said and walked off. I had learned to mistrust all strange men in Egypt, but this was the selfless kindness that Mazen told me had ruled during the uprising.

In deference to the way protest suspended the rules of normal life, Mazen, his friends and I sat on the scuffed plastic chairs of a street teahouse while I recovered. Normally, he hated bustling downtown Cairo with its crowds of lower-middle-class shoppers and workers, and refused to sit with a woman anywhere but in an air-conditioned chain cafe. Listening to them argue about the protests, I realized that now, unlike the single clear goal of getting rid of Mubarak, even they weren't sure what they wanted to achieve.

"The military council must step down," said one.

"There should be a civilian interim authority until we have elections," said another.

"No, that's not practical now," said a third. "First we need rights for the martyrs of the eighteen days and their families."

"We just have to show them that we've tasted freedom now and they can't crush us like they did before," said Mazen.

That week, around fifty protesters were killed. The clashes petered out, leaving downtown Cairo blocked with towering concrete barricades and another set of martyrs' faces—some idealized, some grotesquely distorted by torture—graffitied on its walls.

This time, few cared about their deaths. The protesters in central Cairo were an isolated minority—far smaller even than the minority that had taken to the streets against Mubarak. Most Egyptians were tired of upheaval and terrified by the nosediving economy. Tourism, which before the revolution had supported more than a tenth of the workforce, had collapsed. And Tahrir Square—however symbolic it seemed to the protesters, and however much energy they expended in "defending" it from the security forces—had already become irrelevant. The real struggle for power was taking place off the streets, as Egypt prepared for its first ever free parliamentary elections—a tussle between the tens of new parties, fronts and alliances that had mushroomed in the place of Mubarak's dissolved ruling party. The revolutionaries, stalled in Tahrir, were failing to reach out to the majority of Egypt beyond.

The force rising fastest was a profoundly conservative one. The immediate popularity of the Muslim Brotherhood wasn't surprising. For decades, they had offered the only consistent opposition to the regime. But the rise of the Salafis had caught everyone off-guard.

The Salafis had lived in the shadow of state control and harassment since the 1970s, dismissed by the intelligentsia as manipulators of the poor and credulous. Now, they saw an undreamed-of opportunity for power. I leaned out of my balcony one morning to see thousands of robed and bearded men marching on Tahrir, not a protest so much as a display of force. A group of sheikhs had hastily revised their apolitical principles to form the Nour party, and now Salafi TV channels were rallying the vote for a party with a guarantee of piety, they claimed, even purer and far more disinterested than the Brotherhood's.

When I went to visit Nour's two recently appointed, luxuriantly bearded spokesmen in a bleak tower-block complex by the Nile, I found the party's success had caught them by surprise. They hadn't had time to set up a proper office, and they weren't yet sure how to deal with the press either. I waited for an hour on a cling-filmed black leatherette sofa while they prayed.

"Foreign journalists only ever ask us about beer and bikinis," one complained when they finally sat down—carefully avoiding looking at me, as I was a woman. Transferring the beliefs they had nurtured for so long in private into the public sphere was proving more difficult than they expected. Salafi scholars and parliamentary candidates, carried away by the novelty of interviews, had already suggested that the pagan pyramids should be demurely "veiled" in wax, beaches be segregated, and bikinis and alcohol banned.[4] "Beer and bikinis" was a reasonable line of questioning, given how many Egyptians' livelihoods depended on tourism, but the spokesman's face was set resentfully.

"OK, can you explain how you see the relationship between democracy and the sharia?" I asked. Nour were stridently committed to Islamic law, but less outspoken about how it should be introduced.

They looked at each other, stalled and muttered vaguely. "We would not force the people to accept the sharia . . ."

"But it's preferable if they do?"

They looked at each other again. In their eyes there was no comparison. Democracy was man-made, the sharia divine.

"The people of Egypt are religious by nature," one said finally, repeating a maxim I had heard many times. "If, after we educate and improve the society, a majority of the people get to the point where they want the sharia to be implemented, this is democratic."

"But what about non-Muslims? Or anyone else who doesn't want to live under sharia?"

"All religions agree on basic principles, don't they?" the other answered in a reasonable tone. "Don't steal. Don't commit adultery." He reached for an example he assumed I would understand. "Not even a Christian father will allow his daughter to show her skin in the street. So even Christians will have no problem living under the sharia. It's good for everyone, like water is good for everyone."

Mubarak had warned that if he was removed, Egypt would be overrun by Islamists. Salafism was not what the protesters had fought for in the revolution, but it was now the second strongest political force in the country. I walked home under the campaign banners slung across every street. To help illiterate voters, they identified each candidate by their photograph and a randomly assigned symbol—a toothbrush, a star, a camel, a blender, a bunch of grapes, a violin. By law, each party list of six candidates had to include at least one woman. The Nour posters put their single female candidate last, where she was least likely to be elected, and replaced her photograph with a stylized rose. They had only reluctantly fielded any women at all, because many Salafis believed women should not be permitted to vote, let alone run for office.

When the results were announced, the Brotherhood had won more than 37% of the vote. None of the array of small revolutionary or liberal parties that Amal, Amr and Mazen had voted for had managed to win even 10%. But the Nour-led "Islamist bloc" had won 28%. When MPs were sworn in at the beginning of 2012, pledging to "uphold the constitution," some of the Salafis amended their oaths, adding "and apply God's sharia" or "if not in contradiction with God's sharia."[5] Out of 498 elected MPs, only eight were women.[6]

In June 2012, the Brotherhood's Mohamed Morsi became the fifth president of the Arab Republic of Egypt—and its first ever not to be drawn from the military. He had won the final round runoff against a Mubarak-era air marshal and former prime minister, Ahmed Shafiq, by the narrowest of margins, and his supporters were far from being all Brotherhood true believers. Mazen had voted for him in the hope he could clean up politics, Amal out of disgust with everything Ahmed Shafiq stood for, Amr out of the belief that his countrymen needed to see the Brotherhood in power to realize their true— he believed evil and stupid—identity. Mubarak had been sentenced to life imprisonment for failing to prevent the killing of protesters during the revolution. The army appeared keen to wash its hands of the thankless business of governing and retreat to its more profitable business empire. It seemed clear that conservative Islam was the force that would determine the direction of the new Egypt.

It was spending time with Mazen and Ayman that gave me an insight into the attitudes that lay beneath the new popularity of Islamist politics. They both hated the old regime and thought of themselves as revolutionaries—in spirit if not, in Ayman's case, on the streets. They both had a passionate desire for freedom. But for them, religion was far from a restriction or burden—it was a means of liberation.

At the end of the summer of Morsi's election, I moved to an apartment in Mohandiseen, the concrete 1960s middle-class district on the west bank of the Nile where I had lived in the mid-2000s. It was unfashionable, soulless and had a reputation for even worse traffic than the rest of the city—all of which repelled foreigners—and I perversely liked it because of that. My new flatmate was a twenty-six-year-old British Arabic student called Maggie, whose red hair stood out on the street even more than my fair hair, and who was as curious about Cairo as I was. We lived just off one of the huge boulevards that sliced through Cairo. League of Arab Nations Street, lined with car showrooms and fast-food restaurants, ran past the Mostafa Mahmoud mosque onto an informal red-light district where girls in black robes and headscarves and heavy makeup lingered on the pavements in the evenings.

One autumn afternoon, I was sitting with Mazen in a noisy, airless chain cafe nearby—now the excuse of protests had passed, he flatly refused to sit with me in a streetside teahouse—when he spotted someone reading at a nearby table.

"Ayman!" he called.

The young man looked up. I liked his gentle, mournful expression and the way he was concentrating doggedly on his book amid the uproar of the cafe. It was defiantly un-Egyptian behavior.

Ayman had abandoned his extreme Salafi beliefs before the revolution. The impossible standards of purity they imposed had pushed him into a severe depression, and his parents had been forced to act. With medication and counseling, he had realized how isolated he had become. But he was still very devout, and he had met Mazen at one of the endless Islamic classes, lecture series, seminars and self-development courses they each attended. Like Maggie, they were in their mid-twenties, and after the meeting in the cafe the four of us often spent time together. They were too pious to have spent much time in private with foreign women—unlike the smooth multilingual young men who hung around Arabic schools in the hope of snaring a Western girlfriend—but as we were "respectable" they accepted invitations to tea in our flat.

Gradually, an odd friendship developed between us. We politely made sure there was no alcohol lying around, put on another layer of clothing and bit back our sharpest-tongued retorts about gender, sex and religion. They reluctantly accepted that we rode public transport alone at night, ventured beyond middle-class parts of town and defied the laws of nature to live without male protection—but lectured us relentlessly on Egypt and the modes of correct behavior within it. Sometimes we'd show them how to make pizza from scratch, or hire one of the beautiful lateen-sailed feluccas moored along the corniche and sail on the Nile. Not far beneath his polite exterior, Mazen was excitable and fun-loving, capable of whipping himself up into hyperactive frenzies, while Ayman usually kept the serious look I'd first seen in the cafe.

They liked the novelty of getting to know foreigners, and one evening asked me to accompany them to a rooftop party thrown by a German girl Ayman had met. It was one of the rowdy expat parties I rarely went to, where everyone was studying Arabic or interning for the EU or a development agency—two drunk Norwegians DJing from an expensive laptop, trendy francophone Egyptian men with Afros sharing joints with French girls with nose piercings, Latin American girls in bodycon dresses making out with handsome Sudanese translators from the UN, crates of bad Egyptian beer ordered in from a Coptic delivery service, the doorman bribed to look the other way and the neighbors craning, scandalized and titillated, from their balconies.

For once, in this alien environment, I was Ayman and Mazen's island of security and certainty. They flanked me tightly, now less to lecture me than for protection. When Ayman was towed away by the hostess, I greeted some other guests. Turning to include Mazen, I saw him moving rapidly away toward the edge of the balcony.

"Mazen, where are you going?"

"There's someone drinking alcohol right there. I shouldn't be near it." He scuttled sideways again, wincing. "And there's someone over there."

"Most people are drinking," I said. "Do you want to leave?"

But he shook his head and spent the next twenty minutes triangulating himself from drinkers, eyes bulging with horrified fascination. As soon as Ayman reappeared, as solemnly calm as ever, we left, trailing down the stairs past the Quranic texts and blood handprints outside the other apartments, made from the blood of the slaughtered animal at Eid as protection against the evil eye and to bring good luck to the household.

"So what did you think?" I asked Mazen as we walked back to the main road.

He looked downcast. "I didn't think it would be like that." His experimental night out had only confirmed his disgust with young Westerners' lifestyles.

For years, Ayman and Mazen had both spent their spare hours not partying or chasing girls, but studying Quran, Islamic theology, jurisprudence, philosophy and *mantiq*, or logic. Often, they would share the results with me and Maggie. One evening, when the four of us met in a restaurant that served an Egyptianized rendition of Cantonese food, Ayman gestured around us at the middle-class families struggling with their unfamiliar chopsticks.

"People like us were brought up in a Westernized way, let's say 80% Westernized," he said. "We went to English-language schools, we watched American TV, all that stuff. And many people just continue on that path. But why should we adopt the mindset of the West? As far as I'm concerned there are three mindsets: Western, Eastern and religious. The first two are both rubbish, both bad in their own ways. That leaves the religious mindset."

"Hold on a minute, what are the Western and Eastern mindsets?" asked Maggie.

"You know this," Ayman said patiently. He was used to our skeptical questions and didn't even roll his big mournful eyes. "Western—do anything you want, no boundaries, make money, exploit women, consume. Eastern—oppress women, corruption, ignorant traditions, stuck in the past."

"So how do you know what is the right religious mindset?" I asked. "There's a lot of competition."

"God put something inside you that will guide you to the truth, if you're seeking it sincerely," he said, digging into a plate of chicken and rice. "What we need to do is get back to the foundation. Lay all our beliefs aside and start with pure logic. Then we know we're not being influenced by our culture, by superstition, emotion or anything else."

"This is the kind of stuff that will really blow your mind, the answers to all the big questions," Mazen chipped in excitedly. "Have you got a pen and paper?" I handed him a biro and notebook, and he shoved aside his plate and started to sketch. "There are two things in Islam, *el-aql*, reason, and *el-naql*, evidence, which is the holy texts," he said as he drew. His forehead was furrowed with concentration. "In this case, we're using pure *aql*. We're not just memorizing answers to some questions, we are starting without a final answer in mind." He pushed the paper toward us with a flourish. I looked at the chain of rectangles snaking across the page, each joined to the next by a skinny line.

"What are they?" Maggie asked.

"Extension boards, multi-plug boards," said Mazen. "It's an extension board which is plugged into an extension board which is plugged into another and so on and so on." He looked at Maggie. "Now. Will there ever be any power in the last board if the first one isn't plugged into the wall?"

"Um, no?"

"And if the first extension board is just plugged into itself, will it have any power?"

"I guess not."

Mazen looked triumphant. "Exactly," he said. "Creation needs to get the original power from somewhere. And that somewhere must be God. Now do you see?"

We looked at the lines and rectangles. "Actually, I'm an atheist," said Maggie. I expected Mazen and Ayman to be irritated, if not horrified, at this announcement. But Ayman's eyes lit up at the prospect of a debate he knew he had already won.

"So you are arguing that something—the universe—came out of nothing. This is totally illogical. Where do you think the universe came from?"

"I don't know, to be honest," she said, and he raised his eyebrows triumphantly.

"OK, so you're satisfied to not know," he said. "I need an answer for everything, and my beliefs give me one that is totally logical."

Ayman and Mazen's lives were a whirl of instability. Their parents' values could no longer guide them, their country was in upheaval, and their future was uncertain. Islam was their rock in the middle of the chaos.

"Because we believe in another life, we accept all sorts of restrictions on our behavior that you Westerners don't," said Mazen, cracking open a soda. "If I give up things in this life, I'll have them in the next, but so much better. Like"—he gestured with his soda can—"if I don't drink alcohol in this life, I'll drink something much more delicious in heaven." I knew that apart from its detailed descriptions of the beautiful modest virgins who awaited believers in paradise, the Quran promised them that they would enjoy "rivers of wine delicious to the drinkers."

"OK, you want society to be run like this, but what about people who don't?" I asked.

"Well, each individual should be governed by his religious laws—Muslims by the sharia, Christians by church law, and so on."

"What if he or she doesn't believe in these laws at all, or doesn't believe in the way they are interpreted?"

Mazen shot me a severe look. "Then you are looking at a state of anarchy," he said. "Getting rid of religion leaves you with a very serious problem—regulating human behavior. How do you know what's right or wrong if there are no absolutes? Today you in the West have allowed gay marriage, tomorrow what's to stop you allowing incestuous marriages or eating human meat? I honestly don't understand why secular people like you don't just go down the street shooting people and stealing stuff and—and doing whatever you want. What's to stop you?"

Maggie and I started to talk simultaneously about compassion and shared moral values and respect for life and property. Mazen cut us off.

"It's simple," he said. "If I didn't believe in Judgment Day, I'd blow this whole place up."

I looked at the ornamental fish struggling in their too-small aquarium and the waiters in their shabby mock-Chinese outfits, then out of the window at the bakery, the bookshop, the shwarma grill and the old-fashioned fruit and vegetable shop with its name picked out in beautiful 1930s-style Arabic calligraphy. There was garbage rotting at the curb, a beggar with a swollen leg on the pavement and feral dogs were fighting over the scraps from the shwarma grill.

As we walked back to the metro Mazen's mood lifted and he started chatting with Ayman about Grand Theft Auto. I was surprised. The video game seemed like the epitome of everything they hated about the West—amorality, greed and violence, and sexual excess.

"You play GTA? But what about the women in bikinis? The strippers? The prostitutes? How is that Islamic?" I asked.

They looked at each other. "Er, it's OK because they're not real, it's just a picture," Mazen said. He didn't sound very convincing. We all started to laugh.

"So could you draw a picture of a naked woman? Islamically speaking?" Maggie asked.

"Er, I don't think so, I'm not sure," said Ayman, giggling. "We'll have to ask a sheikh."

Listening to Mazen and Ayman explain their beliefs discouraged me. I could not see how upholding Islam as the sole model for human behavior could create a more fair and open society in Egypt—particularly for women. How would an unconventional, independent woman like Amal fare under an Islamist government that did not believe in secular formulations of women's rights? But the young men brushed aside my concerns.

"You should ask Fadel Soliman to explain about how Islam benefits women," Mazen told me. "He's the person who can best answer you."

A former Muslim Brother, Fadel Soliman had set up his own youth organization, Bridges Foundation, to "correct misconceptions" about Islam. Mazen volunteered for it and I had met Fadel Soliman a couple of times. He had lived and worked in the United States, spoke good English and was always courteous and affable, though his teaching style was as polemical as a tough university lecturer's.

Two weeks later, I arrived at a conference center for a Bridges seminar that would train young Muslims—in English—to counter criticisms of Islam that might be made by non-Muslims. I'd already seen a video about the foundation that gave a barrage of authoritative-sounding facts and statistics. *Our information videos make 97% of the people who leave Islam return to it. Out of every two hundred non-Muslims we present to, one person will probably accept Islam. More women join Islam than men, and 90% of women who join Islam say "it gives me more freedom."*

About 150 young people had gathered at round white-draped tables, men on one side of the room, women on the other. Everyone was good-looking, clean-cut and cheerful, and the air hummed with a hybrid of English and Arabic, the lingua franca of Cairo's educated elite. On each table was a printed sign bearing the name of one of the Companions of the Prophet. I joined a group of young women at "Sayyidina Hassan ibn Thabit," Muhammad's court poet who, tradition related, had lived to the age of 120 and brought Islam to China. One was prodding anxiously at her iPhone, flicking the pages of a Quran app whose ornate calligraphy looked strange on the minimalist screen.

Excited voices rose on the other side of the room, and I looked over to where Fadel Soliman, a bear-like bearded man in his forties, was greeting a crush of young men all jostling to shake his hand. Then he leaped up on the stage.

"Let's start. Was Prophet Muhammad a pedophile for marrying Lady Aisha when she was nine? How do you respond to this allegation? Take three minutes, go!"

"One minute left!" he shouted as voices rose in disagreement and the young women hurriedly checked their Quran apps for relevant quotations. Hands started to shoot up. He picked a shy-looking young woman in a green headscarf. She blushed.

"At the time it was normal, it was something cultural, it was not forbidden, I don't think it was a bad thing . . ." she answered uncertainly, trailing off under his gaze.

He cut her off. "Listen. We are talking about a different era. But in New Hampshire, today, the age of marriage starts at thirteen years old, with the consent of their parents. In Texas, fourteen years old. In Missouri and Mississippi, fifteen years old. In Canada, a hundred years ago, it was eleven years old. It's unfair to judge people according to today's laws and customs." The young women on my table leaned forward, nodding. One was taking notes in a round schoolgirlish English hand, one was recording on her iPhone.

"OK, now let's discuss polygyny. Sharia allows men to have up to four wives, but women can have only one husband. How can you prove to someone from the West that this is something that is not that bad actually, and it can solve problems? Three minutes—go!"

The young women's faces twisted as they thought. They knew Islamic law permitted it, but in Egypt's educated classes multiple marriage was generally frowned upon, considered backward and demeaning. Few middle-class city women were willing to be a man's second wife, or for their husband to marry again. Fadel Soliman frowned as several men's hands went up. "I'm a feminist, I want to hear from women on this one!" he joked and everyone laughed.

"Children should know who their father is," offered one young woman.

"Before Islam men could actually marry more women, so it was cutting the number down," said another.

"It's in the nature of men to have more than one woman, but not in women's nature to have more than one man," said a third.

"Right!" said Fadel Soliman. "It's a question of nature. But how can you prove this?" Everyone looked blank.

"It's simple," he said. "If there's a man who cheats on his wife, even in a Muslim country, he'll go into work and boast to all of his colleagues. He's regarded as a hero. But if a woman cheats even on her—*boyfriend*," he emphasized the word with distaste, "in an atheistic Western society, she won't tell anyone, not even her closest girlfriend, because it's disgraceful for a woman to have more than one man. Men think about sex three to five times a day, women think about it three to five times a month. Of course I'm generalizing a bit here."

I felt fury rising in my throat, but Fadel Soliman's observations were accepted without comment. "Why is the number of wives set at four?" asked a young woman near the front.

"Why four? I don't know exactly, but Allah's wisdom is behind this. Perhaps it's that every woman has her monthly menses for a week, each month, so if there are four, there's always at least one available to the husband."

The young women on my table dutifully copied the point down in their notebooks. No one looked outraged or even surprised at this portrait of women as mere receptacles.

"So why didn't Adam have more than one Hawa?" asked another young woman, using the Muslim name for Eve.

"Not all men marry more than once," Fadel Soliman replied brusquely. Then his voice became persuasive again. "But think about it—every adult woman is ready for marriage, but not every adult man is, because of finances. Perhaps 10% of men are. In Saudi Arabia the percentage might be different, because they're richer, perhaps 50% of men are. Who's going to marry the rest of the women? It solves problems. OK—let's announce the winners!" He gave a bar of Toblerone to the table with the most right answers.

I left the conference hall feeling ambivalent. I knew that Fadel Soliman was intelligent and eloquent. He put forward detailed arguments, minutely referenced from the Quran and

Hadiths, against the violent extremism that might tempt young Muslims looking for inspiration online. He was a staunch opponent of al-Qaeda and had recorded a video refuting the Yemeni sheikh Anwar al-Awlaki's ruling that it was Islamically legitimate to target Western civilians with hijackings and bombings.[7] This kind of opposition to radicalization was far more likely to be successful than any intervention by a secular authority. He was moderate, open to dialogue and debate, and exactly the kind of Islamic teacher with whom non-Muslims could engage.

At the same time, the ideas of women's subordination to men I had just heard him elaborate so bluntly filled me with anger—especially when they were dictated to young women by yet another older man in a position of power and authority. But I realized that my feelings were not shared by anyone else in the audience. No one was coercing the enthusiastic young women at my table—in fact they had all paid a large fee to attend the seminar. The revolution might have done away with Mubarak and loosened the grasp of the police, but another crop of patriarchal figures—religious, bureaucratic and military—had sprung up to take their place.

With the Brotherhood in power, Islamists from ultraconservatives to moderates were determined to leverage deep-rooted belief like Mazen and Ayman's for political gain. Amr Khaled was one of them, aiming with his newly launched Egypt party to transform the popularity of Life Makers into an unstoppable political youth movement. But the revolution had not gone smoothly for him so far. Caution ingrained in him by long years of cat-and-mouse with state security, he had waited until the uprising against Mubarak was almost over to speak out in support of the young protesters. It had cost him much of his hard-won credibility.

"He didn't say anything when we were being shot and tear-gassed by the regime," said Mazen bitterly. He had adored Amr Khaled. "He waited until it was safe to speak out."

I wasn't sure whether Amr Khaled could survive the bumpy transition from faith to politics that had already proven challenging for the Salafis and the Brotherhood. In November 2012 I went to the Life Makers headquarters in the desert suburb of 6th of October City to meet the brains behind the organization and the cofounder of the Egypt party, a middle-aged former senior Muslim Brother called Mohamed Yehia.

With the withdrawal of the police from the streets[8] and the escape—or deliberate release—of thousands of prisoners, crime had soared since the revolution. The highway between Cairo and 6th of October City had become notorious for armed robbery and carjacking. Car theft, kidnappings and sexual assaults by taxi drivers were increasing. Packs of motorcycle thieves worked central Cairo, snatching mobile phones and bags. Middle-class people were afraid of crime in a way they had never been before, and some had begun to mutter nostalgically about the security of Mubarak's police state. On a bus near my home one lunchtime, I was set on by a gang of men and women, the women in face veils, who held me down while they wrenched away my bag, then pushed me out of the open door of the bus. When I reported the theft at the local police station, a man bleeding from the head howled from a cage in the center of the room as impassive officers smoked and ate chicken shwarma sandwiches at their desks, brushing ash and grease off their paperwork. Eventually, an officer produced two ancient, yellowing ledgers with ordinary passport photos pasted into them. Most of the women were wearing face veils.

"It was her, wasn't it?" he said, pointing at random to a photo that looked like it had been taken in 1985.

"She's wearing niqab, you can't see anything," I protested, peering at the tiny image.

He shrugged. "It was probably her then," he said, jabbing at another picture. "We know those gangs that work the buses. The drivers are in on it." Humiliated in the revolution, the police, I had heard from others, now enjoyed seeing citizens suffer from crime. "Let your revolution get your car back for you," one friend had been told. After that, when I went out alone I carried a pepper spray, feeling stupid at the useless gesture. Though it was technically illegal, when security guards discovered it in my bag they let me keep it "because of the situation in the country."

"Yes, times are difficult," Mohamed Yehia agreed when he ushered me into the Life Makers office. He was a neat middle-aged man in a polo shirt and chinos, with intelligent, guarded eyes and a reputation as a cutthroat businessman. "Egyptians are desperately searching for an identity," he said as he settled behind his desk. "They don't know whether they should be Islamic, democratic, liberal, or what. With the Egypt party we are telling them they don't need to look for an identity, because we're all Egyptian. And Egyptians are religious by nature, by identity."

It was a familiar general line, but I knew Mohamed Yehia had more specific allegiances. Because he was a former senior Brother, I expected him to be happy that his onetime colleagues were in power. "So are things improving now that Morsi is the president?" I asked him.

"The Brotherhood aren't using violence, they're using democracy, but the word is 'using,'" Mohamed Yehia said. "Using is different from believing. They are using democratic actions to pursue a fundamentalist vision."

"What vision?" I asked. I was amazed that he was criticizing the Brotherhood in language I had only ever heard secular activists use.

Mohamed Yehia looked at me as though I were stupid. "The dream of the supremacy of Muslims," he replied.

"But—trying to return to the fundamentals of Islam, you consider that a positive aim, no?" I had never heard a devout Egyptian Muslim question the idea of attempting to return to the time of the Prophet, when Islam was by definition pure and perfectly applied. I knew Ayman and Mazen, for instance, would be horrified at the idea of doing so.

Mohamed Yehia wasn't fazed. "Do you see values as permanent, or as changing with time?" he asked coolly. "If values can never change, if all the humans in the world don't have the authority to progress, this is fundamentalism." What the twenty-first-century Brotherhood didn't realize, he thought, was that the world had changed. "Time flows downstream, it's not going to flow upstream. No way. We're now in the twenty-first century, and there are new ideas, development, increasing sophistication. If they want to be left out, it's their choice."

"But you were a Brother for most of your life," I said. I knew Mohamed Yehia had trained alongside all the current leaders of the Brotherhood. "If these 'fundamentalist' ideas are so wrong, why do they appeal to intelligent people?"

"This is the result of despair," he answered. "After the continuous defeats and humiliations that we Arabs have experienced, people can't bear their situation any longer and they can't think of a solution. So they say OK, in years gone by we were living in a much better situation, why don't we go back to that time?"

Rather than harking back to an unobtainable past, what Egypt's young people needed, Mohamed Yehia thought, was to channel their wasted energy into building their future. So in the mid-2000s, he had devised Life Makers and recruited Amr Khaled as its public face.

"Youth are a huge percentage of our population," he said. "Life Makers projects—teaching literacy, recycling, working against drugs—demonstrate their own ability to them. Instead of listening to Amr Khaled telling them they can do anything, they see for themselves that they can achieve miracles."

"And then?" I asked.

"Life Makers develops community leaders, people in their twenties. Don't these same people, when they are in their forties, deserve to be members of parliament and ministers and governors? My role is to establish a political party for them, after they 'graduate' from Life Makers. When they reach this stage of their lives, there will be another batch of young people in Life Makers." For the first time, Mohamed Yehia's chilly facade cracked into an uncalculated smile. "Is it clear now, the vision is clear?" he asked. "Everything is there for a purpose."

Mohamed Yehia's plan had finally brought the political subtext of Amr Khaled's charming televangelism before the revolution out into the open. I didn't know whether it would succeed. But Mohamed Yehia's criticism of the Brotherhood seemed increasingly accurate. In the few months since his election, Morsi's image as a man of the people was fast unraveling. He excluded liberals and youth movements from decision-making, and seemed ever more in thrall to the Brotherhood's religious leadership. His "Hundred days promise" to restore security and fix problems from waste disposal to fuel shortages had failed, and tourism and foreign investment had not yet recovered. And while forging ties with Qatar, a longtime supporter of the Brotherhood, and Turkey, which under Recep Tayyip Erdogan had its own sympathetic Islamist government, he had antagonized the regional powerbrokers in Saudi Arabia and the UAE, where the Brotherhood was banned out of fear of its popularity.

Now, Morsi had just granted himself the power to issue decisions and laws that could not be revoked by any other entity, along with the power to use all "necessary measures and procedures" to protect the January 25 revolution and national unity. The wording of the decree was deliberately vague and sweeping. It seemed as if their opponents' worst fears about the Brotherhood—that they would seek to establish their own theocratic dictatorship—were coming true.

Liberal Egyptians, as well as onlookers in the West, raised fearful comparisons with the Iranian revolution of 1979. Would Egypt's uprising usher in decades of authoritarian Islamic rule? The Iranian Shia regime had only recently repressed its own "Green" pro-reform protest movement, which in 2009 had mustered the largest street demonstrations since 1979. But in the Arab Spring uprisings it saw a chance to topple its rival Sunni regimes in the Gulf, particularly that of its arch enemy Saudi Arabia. It hailed the uprisings in Egypt, Tunisia and Yemen—but not in its ally Syria—as "an Islamic awakening."[9] "The Arab revolutions are inspired by the spirit and model of the Islamic revolution in Iran and they are thus a continuation thereof," Iran's spiritual leader Ali Khamenei had said in a sermon in February 2011.

Many ordinary Egyptians were also disappointed with the Brotherhood. They hadn't seen any of the benefits—jobs, fairer wages, improved services or greater national prosperity—they had hoped would follow the revolution. Others were shocked by the greed and ambition of men they had once regarded as *betou' rabenna*, God's people. In March 2012, a Salafi MP had been forced to resign after it emerged the facial injuries he had claimed he sustained in a carjacking were in fact the result of a nose job at an expensive Cairo hospital. Three months later, a married, middle-aged Salafi MP was sentenced to prison after being discovered committing an "indecent act" in a parked car with a fully veiled teenage girl he claimed was his niece.[10]

There was another, smaller group of disillusioned people. Though Islam might be a central part of their lives, many Egyptians hearing hard-line scholars on the Salafi channels spouting sectarian hatred, advocating lowering the legal age of marriage to nine and abusing liberals in filthy language were shocked.[11] Online, young people from both Muslim and Christian backgrounds gathered to share books by Richard Dawkins and critique religion. A few began to question the very foundations of their faith.

I met Abu el-Hassan in Luxor at the end of 2012, because I had sunstroke again. However long I stayed in Egypt, I couldn't conquer my inbuilt English vulnerability to the desert heat and sun. It was incomprehensible and hilarious to most Egyptians, who never used sunblock or a hat and insisted on wearing vests under their clothes even when the temperature climbed above 104 degrees. Sunstroke was dramatic—a blinding headache was quickly followed by collapse, vomiting and a struggle to breathe as my temperature soared and my grasp on consciousness faltered—and I usually ended up on a drip in hospital. This time, I'd taken a few days' break in Luxor and was enjoying being a tourist, crisscrossing the desert between the empty tourist-abandoned temples on a small red Chinese motorbike. But a careless ten minutes in the winter sun, and I was sick again. The international clinic sent a Salafi doctor to hang a drip over the light fitting in my hotel room and, the next day, Abu el-Hassan to check up on me.

Abu el-Hassan was a lean, elegant twenty-eight-year-old with long delicate fingers, who had trained as a gastroenterologist and spent the past three years working in the hotels of the Red Sea coast, treating elderly Germans for holiday diarrhea, before moving to Luxor. When he'd finished and dressed my hand, he sat opposite me and we started to talk.

"I'm a *hafez*," he said eventually. "I can recite the whole Quran from memory, all five hundred pages of it. All because when I was this high"—he gestured the height of a three-year-old—"my father sent me to learn it."

A *hafez* was a living carrier of the word of God. According to the Hadiths, his intercession could save seven sinful relatives from hellfire and clothe his parents in eternal robes worth more than the possessions of a king. But Abu el-Hassan no longer believed any of this. He was an atheist, he confessed.

To identify yourself as an atheist was to invite both total social rejection and physical danger. Earlier that year, a young Christian-born atheist blogger called Alber Saber had called police for protection when an Islamist mob surrounded his house and threatened his family. He was arrested, abused in detention and sentenced to three years in prison.[12] The battle against atheism went right to the heart of the establishment. I'd recently met Amr Sherif, a courtly sixty-something who combined his role as professor of general surgery at Ain Shams University with writing books "scientifically" refuting atheism. His latest, *The Myth of Atheism*, referenced a dizzying array of Western sources: Kant, Carl Sagan, Karl Popper, Wittgenstein, Aristotle, Darwin, Auguste Comte, *Zen and the Art of Motorcycle Maintenance*, Xenophanes, *The Selfish Gene*, the astronomer Martin Rees, the astrophysicist Guillermo Gonzalez, Robert Zemeckis (the director of *Back to the Future*) and Hobbes. The three conclusions he drew from this evidence were, he said, rigorously logical: God existed, he communicated with humanity, and Islam was the one true faith.

Early the next year, Abu el-Hassan moved back to Cairo to study German and take advanced medical courses in preparation for emigrating to Germany. In spring 2013 he invited me to visit his family home, and I found myself sitting in a battered microbus weaving toward Abu Zaabal, a semirural, semi-industrial area on the northern fringes of Cairo famous for its prison and ceramics factories. The local men squashed in around us were wearing blue and black country-style robes or cheap slacks and shirts, and Abu el-Hassan looked obviously out of place with his pristine jeans and laptop case.

Like many areas far from the city centers, Abu Zaabal was very religious. Men from the village had gone to fight the Soviets in Afghanistan in the 1980s, two of Abu el-Hassan's uncles had been imprisoned for suspected links to jihadi groups, and everyone wanted their sons to memorize the Quran. From the age of three, Abu el-Hassan had been sent to a madrasa where boys were beaten into learning the entire text, sitting in rows before the sheikh as they had for hundreds of years. But as he grew into a teenager, being a good Muslim felt harder. He was exhausted by the guilt whenever he thought about girls or sneaked a cigarette from a classmate. He started to think the Quran was riddled with inconsistencies and inaccuracies. After he graduated from medical school, he decided, in secret, that he no longer believed in Islam.

"Islam is a 3D religion," he said now in the microbus, as the burned-sugar smell of the driver's tobacco curled around us. He was speaking English in a low voice so the other passengers couldn't overhear. "This is something very clever about its design. They made hell and heaven so vivid that you can see them clearly in your imagination. My whole life, I believed there are two angels sitting one on each of my shoulders, recording everything I did. There's nothing you think, say or do that they don't record. And I had this belief ever since I could think."

"How did you get rid of it?" I asked.

"People push things that don't fit down into their subconscious," he said. "Gradually, they push down more and more, and some people still have room, but I didn't. And one day, it just burst out of me. I couldn't believe any more. And I realized I could get rid of the belief without losing myself. But I can't tell the people close to me. For a father to think that his son, his little son, will certainly go to hell—this would take away everything from him."

"So how do you manage?"

"A lot of people who feel the way I do keep praying, keep fasting, keep pretending to be Muslim even though inside they don't believe," he said. "I respect them, because it's so hard here. But for me, I just couldn't do it." He looked out of the window at the fruit and vegetable stands, auto-repair shops and dusty palm trees of the place where he had grown up. "So I had to move away from my family, to work in the tourist resorts, so as not to cause them this pain."

Knowing all this, I didn't know what to expect when I saw Abu el-Hassan with his family. But in a tall red-brick apartment building packed closely with many others, he was greeted lovingly by his grandmother, his four younger sisters and brothers, his mother and his father, a tall, dignified schoolteacher in a flowing gray robe. While his mother and sisters prepared dinner, Abu el-Hassan took me to see the view over Abu Zaabal, up a narrow, uneven concrete staircase that twisted through a stairwell open to the sky. We picked our way over piles of dusty red bricks and bundles of steel rebars. On the half-finished top floor, six turkeys were scratching about in a roofless room with a piece of plywood wedged across the empty doorway. It was a little island of farmyard marooned in the fast-growing sprawl of the city.

"This is where I should be living," said Abu el-Hassan, looking at the birds and laughing. It was customary for generations of Egyptian families to live all together in the same building. As the eldest son, Abu el-Hassan should have moved into his own apartment on the roof, with a wife and children, years ago. Instead, he was single and finishing the paperwork for his emigration to Europe. "They ask me, 'If you don't live here, who is going to live here?' I tell them, 'The turkeys.' My mother started to say, 'I don't care who you marry, even an Israeli, but you have to marry!'"

When we all sat on the floor downstairs to eat from a low table, Abu el-Hassan was the honored eldest son. His sisters brought an endless procession of dishes from the kitchen, offering him choice morsels from each, his mother stroked his hair, his littlest brother dashed about in excitement. When the whole family settled on the cushions to drink tea and watch a Turkish soap opera after dinner, it was a picture-perfect scene of middle-class Egyptian life. But Abu el-Hassan, though he loved his family, knew he couldn't stay. Like Amal, to live his life according to his own beliefs, he had to leave them.

No matter how deeply religion was woven into Egyptian society, Morsi's unpopularity was growing, and he seemed unable to turn the tide. In May 2013, I started to hear about a group called Tamarod—Rebel—which was collecting signatures calling on Morsi to step down and hold early presidential elections. It was a collection of the leftist, secular and revolutionary groups and figures that had been so ineffectual in previous elections, but now it was starting to gain traction, recruiting ordinary people to photocopy, distribute and collect copies of its petition. "Because the streets remain insecure, we don't want you. Because the poor still have no place, we don't want you. Because the economy has collapsed and is based on begging, we don't want you," it read.[13]

Amal, the English teacher from the Fayoum, had overflowing carrier bags of them in her apartment stairwell. Chains of young people stood along the roads outside big shopping malls, restaurants and cafes, handing them out to drivers and passersby. Tamarod's tactics were familiar, seeking to replicate the social media–driven, grassroots campaigns that had helped oust Mubarak a little over two years earlier. It called for a mass protest on June 30, the first anniversary of Morsi's inauguration. But it didn't seem to have a plan for what would happen afterward.

No one could escape the growing sense of crisis. As temperatures rose and the threatened demonstration approached, there was suddenly an acute petrol shortage. Morsi had sent it all to Hamas in Gaza, his opponents alleged, while officials blamed smugglers and black marketeers. Main streets were blocked with queues for petrol stations, drivers sitting in their cars for hours while entrepreneurial street vendors hawked snacks and cold drinks and set up shisha pipes by the car doors. The Egyptian pound slipped even further against the dollar. A Salafi-led lynch mob murdered four Shia in a Giza village street after months of sectarian incitement which Morsi's government had done nothing to curb. There were interminable power cuts during which everyone sweated angrily in the dark.

When the power flickered on, Morsi made a televised speech to the nation that began late, lasted for hours and alternately shocked and bored people to hysteria.

"I have made mistakes," he conceded, then launched a threatening diatribe against a series of public figures including media moguls and his former presidential competitor Ahmed Shafiq, who he claimed were conspiring against him.[14] Still, no one knew what would happen on June 30.

"Nothing will happen," people said.

"It's going to be huge," others said. It felt, as Tamarod intended, like January 25, 2011.

In the end, on June 30, huge crowds turned out to protest against Morsi, with smaller numbers staging counterprotests to support him. People knew exactly what to do, as if they were acting out their memories of the 2011 revolution. As I drove through the city, I saw the same long, banner-like

Egyptian flags that snaked above the heads of hundreds of people, the same placards and face paint, the same chants of "Leave." Tamarod said that 33 million had taken to the streets across Egypt; others claimed 14 million; others hundreds of thousands.[15] The next day, the army imposed a forty-eight-hour deadline for the president to "meet the people's demands" and the crowds came back out to celebrate. The Brotherhood, the army and Tamarod all denied that the statement amounted to a military coup. But in place of the police bullets that had met the 2011 protesters, the state news agency reported that the police were handing out free bottled water and juice to marchers. Army helicopters trailing Egyptian flags flew over the crowds in Tahrir, who screamed with joy, pinpointing each one with hundreds of green laser beams. Meanwhile, the headquarters of the Muslim Brotherhood were looted and burned.

Three days later, on July 3, security forces took Morsi and his senior aides into military custody. General Abdel Fattah el-Sisi, whom Morsi had appointed defense minister less than a year earlier, appeared on television flanked by the grand imam of al-Azhar, the Coptic pope, the liberal politician Mohamed ElBaradei, and the leader of the Salafi Nour party, and announced to the nation that the army was instituting "a new road map" for Egypt. Immediately after the announcement, Islamist TV channels that might be sympathetic to Morsi all went off the air. Brotherhood leaders were rounded up and jailed, just as they had been under Mubarak. As crowds celebrated, the air force display team trailed the colors of the Egyptian flag and drew a heart in the sky over Tahrir. Defying the revolutionaries and the Islamists alike, riding on a wave of protest led by liberals who didn't understand that power no longer rested in the hands of the people, the army was back.

6

Ruqayah and Sara:
The Generals Return

Ruqayah crouched behind a sandbag wall on the petrol station forecourt, blinking away the sweat running into her eyes. The sun was directly overhead and the acrid smell of burning plastic stung the back of her throat. Shouts and screams rose thinly over gunfire, helicopter rotors and the rumble of armored bulldozers. Beside her huddled another teenage girl and a young man, pressed as close as they could to the rough burlap. Off to the side, sprawled on the concrete with blood pooling around them, lay the bodies of the two other men who had been with them. The sandbag wall wasn't big enough to shelter them all, and they had been shot dead by police snipers.

"Don't move until I tell you. Then, run," the man told the two girls. Ruqayah nodded silently and waited, closing her eyes, clasping the other girl's hand, for the brief silence that meant the shooters were reloading. She knew to bend double and run in zigzags to make herself a harder target. When she opened her eyes she saw other people, adults, teenagers and small children, crouching in the angle of walls, against cars, behind rough barricades of paving stones, anything that would protect them from the gunfire coming from the square and the snipers on the rooftops around them. Then one man, bearded and strongly built, stood up and spread his arms wide in defiance, facing the square.

"I won't crawl," he shouted. *"Allahu Akbar!"* Ruqayah squeezed her eyes shut again, but she still heard his skull shatter around the sniper's bullet.

"Now!" the young man told them and they dashed behind him, weaving left and right, for the shelter of a side-street. Ruqayah was just fifteen, wiry and fleet, but the other girl was older and heavier. A bullet caught her in the leg and she fell as Ruqayah watched in horror from the side-street. The girl crawled the last yards to them, leaving a trail of blood.

It was the middle of August 2013, soon after the Eid feast that marked the end of Ramadan, and the security forces were clearing the pro-Morsi protest camps at Rabaa and al-Nahda squares in central Cairo. Ruqayah had been living in the larger Rabaa camp for six weeks, since joining the protest in support of the president on June 30, a counterweight to the huge Tamarod marches against him that had converged in Tahrir. They were citizens too, they had voted for Morsi in free and fair elections, she reasoned—or at least those of them who were over eighteen and didn't have to go to school had—why shouldn't they go out to defend their democratic rights? Street protest had worked in Tahrir in 2011, and the world had hailed it as an inspiring expression of democracy. After the revolution, the power should lie in the hands of the people. Why not in Rabaa too?

Besides, some of Ruqayah's family and friends were members of the Brotherhood, others sympathized with them, and all were witnesses to the military state's long years of torture, imprisonment and surveillance of Islamists. The protesters at Rabaa were her people and it was her duty to help them. With other high-school and university students, she volunteered at the checkpoints at the camp's perimeter, checking handbags and IDs as women entered in the gender-segregated lines, patting them down for hidden weapons or explosives. Her post was at the camp's western edge where a cross-street met Nasr Road, which ran on past their makeshift paving-stone barricades to the parade stand where Sadat had been assassinated in 1981 and the elevated 6th of October highway that led to downtown Cairo.

Ruqayah had turned fifteen the day the army arrested Morsi. She was a quiet, studious girl whose family had sent her to an al-Azhar Islamic high school, part of the parallel semi-private education system administered by the country's highest Islamic authority. On the morning of July 3, she had finished her last algebra exam and gone straight to work on her checkpoint at Rabaa. By late evening she was exhausted, but she stayed awake with the other volunteer guards to listen to the promised military statement on an old radio. Ruqayah wasn't worried. God promised injustice would never triumph, and Morsi was their rightful president. God would never let him be removed like the tyrant Mubarak.

"By God's will everything will be fine," she told her friends confidently, and they cheered her and agreed.

But as soon as she heard General Sisi's first words, she knew it was a military coup. Around her young men sank to their knees, crying and begging God for help. Ruqayah had never seen these men who always seemed so strong and lion-like, towering over her and calling her "little sister," look weak and humiliated. At midnight, they heard shooting in the darkness as security forces surrounded the camp, sealing it off from the rest of Cairo. It was the first time she had ever heard live gunfire. She dropped to her knees in fear, reciting Quranic verses and praying for God to protect them.

The military takeover had given Egypt another "revolution," this one state-authorized. June 30, the day of the huge anti-Morsi protests, was now described as "the new January 25." Since Misr 25 and other Islamist channels had been closed down, Egyptian media was almost entirely pro-army, broadcasting endless hours of patriotic messages and vilification of Morsi and the Brotherhood. The majority of Egyptians, numbed into pragmatism by eighteen months of upheaval, seemed grateful for the return of military rule. But there were many—led by the Muslim Brotherhood but including other Islamists, leftists and liberals—who weren't, whether they had supported Morsi or not. The camps at Rabaa and al-Nahda, organized and led by the Brotherhood, were their strongholds. By early August, Rabaa was home to an estimated eighty-five thousand protesters from across the country, housed in a sprawling makeshift city more than half a mile across.[1]

In the middle of the sit-in, I went to visit Rabaa. It was the fasting month of Ramadan and as mercilessly hot as a desert city in high summer could be. The army had blocked all the roads leading to the camp so I walked the last half mile from the elevated highway, skirting their tanks and weaving through the towering barricades the protesters had built from paving stones and bricks until I reached Ruqayah's checkpoint. As I trudged on in the sun, I doubted that street protests could really withstand the might of a military that this time, unlike its permissiveness of early 2011, was determined to crush them. But few of the protesters shared my misgivings. I had expected the mood in the camp to be somber, but it was as festive as Tahrir in its heyday. As I waited in the women's line for entry, young men patrolled with backpack tank-and-hose kits, misting us with water to keep cool. The women and girls around me, all veiled and clad in heavy robes, were laughing and competing to be sprayed in the face.

Inside, the familiar intersection where I often sat in snarled traffic or changed microbus lines was transformed. At ground level, the scale of the camp was breathtaking. Tents were neatly ranged along the center of the street, tall square constructions of timber and blue plastic sheeting with families lying on mats inside reading the Quran or sleeping until sunset, when they could eat and drink. On the sidewalks, street vendors grilled spits of chicken and sold water pistols, fruit and sunglasses. Banners proclaimed "Morsi is our legal president," "My vote counts" and "Democracy vs. coup." The main stage, in front of the mosque that gave the square and the camp its name, was playing Quranic recitation. The army's supporters said that the Brotherhood had tortured and murdered people in the spaces under the stage, and that they kept caches of weapons and explosives there. Now, there was nothing but a dim, empty expanse of scaffolding.

I'd come looking for Mazen, who spent days in the camp visiting his Brotherhood friends, but he had gone home to break the fast with his mother. So I sat in a homely tent with a group of women, all engineering lecturers and PhD students. They had wired electricity in from a nearby streetlight, set up fans and a small gas burner and hung up a neatly lettered banner reading "Engineers Against the Coup."

"We'll never leave," said a dignified middle-aged woman who taught at a university in the delta. "It's a matter of our rights, dignity and democracy. Why should the army seize the country again, by force?"

"Do you want Morsi to come back?" I asked.

"Yes, that's the only solution we'll accept. He's our only legitimate leader."

"What if he doesn't?"

"We're ready to be martyred here," said a younger woman. "We'd rather die free than live under this injustice. We know God will give us our rights, even if the army won't." The others nodded in agreement. Once you passed the checkpoints on the camp's edge, God, not the army, was the supreme arbiter of earthly politics.

I could never get used to hearing people talk about martyrdom. But after their long history of struggle with the state, it was a central part of the Brotherhood's self-image. Given how many had recently died in protests and detention, it was also far from rhetorical. The army's supporters said that the protesters at Rabaa and al-Nahda were actively seeking death, keeping women and children in the camps as human shields—though no one questioned why peaceful protesters should need "human shields" against their own security forces.[2] The protesters had a different view. Ruqayah was only fifteen, but her parents, who were also in the camp, would rather see their daughter stand up for justice than bow to the hated regime.

But as the weeks rolled on, it was increasingly obvious to all but the most fervent believers that Morsi was never coming back. Since the coup, the army had held him incommunicado at a secret location and the rest of the country had almost forgotten him. To them, Rabaa seemed trapped in time, a fragment of an unworkable past. But to Ruqayah, and to many of those living there with her, it was a Utopia. When she looked around she saw that everything in the camp was purposeful and harmonious, from the communal kitchens to the rota for stage speakers to the construction of tents to the security details that she belonged to. She thought, as Amr and Mazen had thought about Tahrir in 2011, that Rabaa was a miniature model of Egypt's perfect future. To Ruqayah, Rabaa was far more beautiful than Tahrir, because it was guided by the true spirit of Islam. She knew its victory was guaranteed.

To those less romantic than Ruqayah, it was clear that Rabaa was not idyllic. The progressive young Islamists who managed the stage rota and media relations were in despair over the unreconstructed firebrand sheikhs who preached sectarian hatred against Christians and other supposed traitors to Morsi, rather than speaking about democracy and human rights. Mazen shared a joke on Facebook—*Please God, let these sheikhs have the honor of being martyred first.*

Though they claimed their legitimacy stemmed from the mass protests of June 30, Egypt's new leaders had no time for public expressions of anything that threatened their own interests. The camps at Rabaa and al-Nahda, they decided, would not be tolerated. The pressure on Rabaa was stepped up. On July 8 fifty-one protesters were shot dead and more than four hundred injured when a sit-in outside the Republican Guards base near the square, where protesters thought Morsi might be detained, was attacked by security forces.[3] On July 26, Sisi called for a mass public demonstration to give him a mandate to "fight terrorism," and tens of thousands of Egyptians took to the streets in sedate marches once again guarded by the police and army. Street protest, the tool young people had turned to in desperation to take back power from Mubarak's regime, had now been thoroughly co-opted by the state.

"The source of legitimacy is the people," reflected Sisi piously. "The ballot box is a means for legitimacy. If there was any other way than taking to the streets to reject [Morsi's] legitimacy, the people would have taken it."[4]

He didn't extend the same logic to his opponents. The day after the pro–el-Sisi march, around ninety unarmed pro-Morsi protesters were shot dead by security forces on a main street close to Rabaa. Before the Eid feast on August 8, the army-appointed prime minister announced that Rabaa and its smaller twin camp at al-Nahda Square would be cleared by force.

In the early hours of August 14, Ruqayah curled up on a blanket at her post. She had been on duty at the checkpoint on the edge of the camp without a break for two days. Before dawn, her mobile rang.

"The army are breaking into the square," her uncle shouted. His voice was hoarse with panic. "You have to get out."

Ruqayah laughed. "They say this every day, Uncle. Don't worry about it."

Then she heard gunfire in the distance and smelled the faint burn of tear gas on the air. Racing from her post back toward the square, Ruqayah saw armored bulldozers rolling toward it, blunt-nosed armored personnel carriers (APCs) behind them. She found her mother and little sister sheltering in the field hospital, a small hall close to the mosque with makeshift facilities for treating sunstroke and flu. Ruqayah ran back to her post at the boundary. Behind the paving-stone barricades her fellow guards were throwing stones at a line of APCs advancing through a choking cloud of tear gas.

Then the shooting started. As far as Ruqayah knew, everyone in the camp was unarmed, though it later emerged that ten or twenty protesters had firearms.[5] Minutes after the clearance began, soldiers on the ground and snipers on surrounding rooftops were using live ammunition indiscriminately against the entire camp. According to the security forces' plan, the entrance where Ruqayah was stationed was supposed to be a "safe exit" for protesters. As they approached, the army vehicles blared recorded assurances that safe exits would be provided. Brotherhood speakers yelled from the main stage that their promises were lies. "Do not leave!" they urged the protesters. But now it was too late. With the gunfire, gas and careering vehicles there was no chance of escape for anyone.

"Girls get back from the boundary," the men at her post were shouting. "Girls take cover. It's not safe." They wanted to protect her, but Ruqayah refused to move. *This is my gate, my place, the one I'm responsible for*, she thought. *I will never leave it.*

Then her friend Amro fell. For six weeks, they had worked together every day on the checkpoint. She ran forward, shouting, and the men around him parted, thinking in the confusion that a woman on the front lines must be a doctor. As she knelt beside Amro, helplessly watching the blood pumping from bullet wounds in his chest and head, she saw his eyes go blank. It was the first death she had ever seen. It was 7 a.m., less than an hour after the attack on the camp had begun.

By the middle of the day Ruqayah had lost count of the number of people she had seen die. The rain of bullets was stronger than ever, and bulldozers had shoveled their barricades into nothingness, crushing defenders beneath them. She retreated into an empty petrol station nearby with young men she didn't know, who let her stay because they still thought she was a doctor. They had no way to reach the main square, because of the snipers. From behind their sandbags, the men were throwing chunks of paving stones to ward off the vehicles and foot soldiers approaching them.

"We need three martyrs to go to the square and get us more stones," the leader said when their supply was exhausted. Ruqayah noticed dully that he didn't say "guys," as he would normally have done, but "martyrs." The square was a three-part zigzag run away, each leg exposed to sniper fire. The chances of making it there and back alive were minimal.

In the main square, twenty-one-year-old Sara was sheltering in the mosque that gave Rabaa its name. Her fiancé, Karim, a fellow student at al-Azhar University, had rushed her to the mosque for protection, with tens of other women and children. Armored bulldozers were closing from every side, shoveling the burning wreckage of the camp before them.

"Good-bye, sweetheart," Karim said as he left. "May God protect you."

The mosque should have been safe. But now, around Sara, its pillared hall was filling with bodies, men and a few women, as a stream of protesters came carrying the dead. They laid the corpses down in long rows, volunteers binding their jaws, feet and hands with cotton strips, with barely time to finish before the next arrived. The mosque's windows were shut tight against tear gas and in the stifling heat blood was spreading rapidly over the plastic matting. It smelled like a butchery. Sara watched, horrified, as a badly wounded man struggled for breath.

"Say the *shahada!*" the people kneeling around him urged. If a Muslim repeated the Islamic creed as his final words before death, he would go straight to paradise. But the man couldn't. He just gasped until he choked and was silent. Beside Sara crouched a woman with a toddler in her arms, crying "My husband, I want my husband." Each time the men carried another body in, she leaped up to look at its face. But many were too disfigured to identify, their heads pulped by high-velocity bullets. Others were charred into anonymity. The woman fainted.

Sara couldn't bear it any longer. She would rather die outside, where she could breathe. She ran out through the courtyard, dodging the men carrying more bodies, and joined a group of women breaking paving stones for the men to throw. She was small and it was a struggle to even lift the stones from the ground, but anything was better than being in the mosque. Salah Soltan, a senior Muslim Brother who taught at her university, passed her, heading to the mosque. Sara called to him.

"Doctor, how long is this going to last? Won't they leave us alone now?"

He looked at her kindly. "No daughter, they won't. I don't know when it will end."

The attack on the square intensified. Just after midday, she called Karim. When he answered, his voice was very weak.

"What happened? Are you OK?" she asked, a chill running through her.

"Yes, yes, don't worry," he said. "But I was hit by two bullets, one in my stomach and the other in my knee."

"Where are you?"

"I'm in the hospital, on the fifth floor." For the first time, his voice shook. "Everyone around me is dead," he said. There was a small government-owned hospital building with basic facilities behind the mosque, where volunteer doctors and medical workers from the camp were trying to treat casualties. But from early morning, they had been overwhelmed: the ground awash with blood and doctors able to do no more than bandage wounds. Now, snipers on the roof of the traffic authority building next door had made entering or leaving the hospital impossible, even for medical staff. Both casualties on stretchers and ambulance workers themselves had been shot dead.

All Sara could do was sink to the ground and pray as hard as she could for God to save him. Her father and mother, ducking and choking from the tear gas, found her where she was kneeling. They were worried that her sixteen-year-old brother, who had been on the front lines alongside Ruqayah, had been killed. The family trailed from the field hospital back to the terrible mosque and the halls around it, searching through tens, then hundreds, of shot, burned and crushed bodies for Sara's brother.

By late afternoon, the security forces had reached the center of the square. Soldiers were advancing in APCs and on foot, supported by helicopters hovering overhead. Special forces were storming the last of the protesters' footholds: an empty tower block behind the mosque, the hospital and finally the mosque and its courtyard. At 5:30 p.m., there was a lull in the shooting and loudspeakers announced there was a safe exit for protesters to the west, where Ruqayah's checkpoint had once been. With her parents and brother, who they had found alive and unharmed, Sara ran out of the square between jeering rows of soldiers, her head tucked low for fear of bullets. Ruqayah met her mother, dragging her little sister by the hand, at the edge of the square.

"They're evacuating the square, they're evacuating us, we have to leave!" her mother shouted, her face streaked with tears.

"I won't go," said Ruqayah firmly. What could be worse than what she had already seen? "I will never leave."

Her mother, at breaking point, slapped her hard across the face. "How can you say this?" They too ran out, ducking between the soldiers. As they left, the field hospital, the main stage, the mosque and the main hospital were set on fire. Many of the bodies they held were burned.

That night, Sara discovered that Karim had been saved from the hospital in the square. When special forces cleared the hospital in the late afternoon, doctors and medical volunteers were forced to abandon their injured patients, some of whom were executed in front of them. But Karim's friends had managed to drag him to a car and get him admitted to a nearby private hospital. Several other hospitals in the area, afraid of government retribution, had rejected wounded or dead protesters. For the first week after his shooting, he talked to Sara when she visited him, trying to reassure her.

"I love you," he told her cheerfully. "You look so lovely in that dress."

But by the second week, he was delirious and no longer recognized her. The doctors said that it was an infection from the bullet that had pierced his abdomen. On August 30, sixteen days after he had been shot, he died.

I had been overseas during the clearance of the camps, and I returned to a changed city. The army had renewed the state of emergency—which Egypt had lived under almost continuously since 1967—and imposed a dusk-till-dawn curfew. The Cairo I knew didn't sleep, its streets traffic-choked and alive with workers, shoppers and families until the small hours. Now, when I landed after curfew, the streets were still and silent as my approved taxi carried me through the army checkpoints, soldiers looming out of the dark with guns and sniffer dogs to check my ID and search my bags. Coils of razor wire blocked the end of my road, and the owners of the sleazy shisha cafe on the corner, where men from the Gulf sat with suspiciously heavily made-up women until dawn, had planted an ostentatious Egyptian flag in the plant pot that weighed one end of the wire down. Tanks and APCs sat at the intersections, their guns trained down the main streets, their crews drinking glasses of tea brought out by my neighbors. In a middle-class area like Mohandiseen, few wanted to antagonize the army.

There was none of the sense of self-reliance and empowerment that had sprung up after the revolution of 2011. Then, with the police gone from the streets, men had banded together to defend their own neighborhoods and discuss politics while they did it. This time, the country's new rulers had banned people's committees, instructed everyone to observe the curfew and brought neighborhoods back under police control.

The people I was writing about were worn by the stress of the last weeks. Amr rolled his eyes at what he saw as the Brotherhood's self-destructive idiocy, but he looked grim-faced too. The coup against Morsi had cast a shadow over the 2011 revolution—both army-sanctioned, both succeeded by military governments. Was democracy possible in Egypt, he wondered, or would the army always have the final word?

Amal, who had worked so hard for what she thought was the grassroots Tamarod protest movement against Morsi, was sickened by the killings at Rabaa. Morsi's supporters alleged that the Tamarod movement had been orchestrated by the army, and now it was emerging that it had been supported by retired officers and tycoons close to the old regime. The spontaneity and credibility of the huge demonstrations of June 30 were suddenly cast into doubt. Had she just been manipulated by the army?

For a long time, no one was sure how many people had been killed in Rabaa and at the other protest camp in al-Nahda Square. Karim was one of many. Shocking photographs circulated of the bodies lined up in Rabaa mosque and the nearby Iman mosque, but army supporters and even government officials dismissed them as fakes.

"The official number of bodies that came out of Rabaa was forty-something bodies," the interior minister Mohamed Ibrahim told a TV interviewer. "The Brotherhood brought bodies from the governorates to Iman mosque to say these were people who had died in Rabaa."[6] The Brotherhood claimed that up to six thousand had died.[7] Eventually, independent human rights groups estimated that one thousand people had been killed in central Cairo in twelve hours.

The Brotherhood was once again officially banned, and its assets seized by the state. In addition to the eight hundred people arrested during the clearance of Rabaa, the remaining senior Brothers were gradually hunted down, their arrests by masked soldiers screened on state television. Salah Soltan, the professor Sara had met outside Rabaa mosque, was captured at the airport as he tried to catch a flight to Khartoum. Non-Brotherhood Islamists didn't escape the net. Amr Khaled had fled to London. The Egypt party that he and Mohamed Yehia had invested so much hope in had folded, its office closed and shuttered, the sign gone. In a few short months, the Islamists had gone from triumphant masters of Egypt's future to hunted victims of the state.

I tried calling Mazen many times, but he wasn't answering his phone. When he finally came to visit he looked worse than anyone, his skin gray and his eyes ringed with bruise-like shadows. All his playfulness had evaporated. He sat on the edge of our sofa and spoke in a low voice, his eyes fixed on the floor.

"I wasn't there when they cleared Rabaa," he said. He looked ashamed. "There are six optional days you can fast after Ramadan, and I was on my fifth day of fasting, so I was at home, asleep. My dad was in Saudi Arabia, but my mum was at home and so was my half-sister, my dad's daughter with his second wife. My dad found out what was happening, and he called my mum and told her to lock all the doors and hide the keys, so I wouldn't be able to go to Rabaa."

Mazen rarely talked about his family, but I knew that his father spent most of his time in the Gulf. He was still married to Mazen's mother, but he had spent little time with their family since Mazen was small, preferring his second wife and children with her. It was a constant source of pain to Mazen and his mother.

"So you were trapped?" I asked.

"Well, when I woke at 3 p.m. I was surprised that I didn't have any calls from my friends at Rabaa. I switched on my laptop and saw the pictures—the bulldozers, the snipers, the people with their heads broken open and their brains leaking out. I tried to call my friends and their numbers were disconnected. I put on my clothes and ran out of my room. I found the doors locked and my mother hysterical. I couldn't get out. So I opened a window and climbed out, down the side of the building and ran through the streets toward Rabaa."

I winced. Security forces had also shot at anyone trying to help those trapped in the camp.

"My phone rang; it was my father. His second wife had heard I'd gone out of the window and called him in Saudi Arabia to snitch on me, to make trouble for me and my mother. He shouted at me to go back otherwise he'd divorce my mother. This is the way he knew he could hurt me. I said, 'From what you're saying, I can see how you think of me and of my mother,' and I hung up and went on. Then I finally got a call from a friend saying, 'Don't come, don't come, there's nothing you can do. It's all over. The choice is be killed or be imprisoned now, and it's better you stay back. This isn't the final round, there will be another round.'"

"What did you do?"

"What could I do?" Mazen asked bitterly. "I went home. My mother was inconsolable. I found out three of my close friends were dead and more were shot and wounded. This guy we went to visit at the Brotherhood youth office has a bullet lodged in his hip. Do you remember him?" He looked up at me and I nodded. In 2011, when the parties were preparing for the first parliamentary elections after the revolution, Mazen and I had gone to meet the Brotherhood's enthusiastic new officials. It felt like a lifetime ago.

"What will happen now, Mazen?" I asked. I had never seen him look so defeated. He was the perpetual optimist and activist, buoyed up by his unshakable faith. But now he just shrugged.

"I don't know. I just stay at home, sleeping, trying to forget everything that's happened."

*

Rabaa trailed revenge in its wake. Because Copts were assumed to support the regime, in the weeks after the clearance Islamist gangs burned thirty-seven churches and attacked dozens of Christian-owned schools, businesses and homes.[8] The state was also targeted. A lynch mob murdered fourteen police officers in a village outside Cairo. "We will show you rage and we will make you see terrorism," they spray-painted on the nearby church after burning it along with the police station.[9] In north Sinai, militants ambushed and shot dead twenty-five off-duty policemen.[10] A powerful bomb planted in central Cairo narrowly failed to assassinate the interior minister Mohamed Ibrahim, who had overseen the clearance of the camps. It was the city's first major bombing for years and shook Cairenes who prided themselves on their city being no Baghdad or Benghazi. A Sinai-based jihadi group calling itself Ansar Beit el-Maqdis, Champions of Jerusalem, claimed responsibility for the attack.

There was no evidence that the militants were connected to the Brotherhood. But in the sticky gloom of the curfew, with everyone confined unaccustomedly at home all evening, the country was gripped by witch-hunt hysteria. When I turned on the TV, presenters were describing the Rabaa protesters and jihadis alike as "terrorists," "enemy agents" or simply "Brotherhood." It was no surprise that Egypt's corrupt and conservative media was so easily controlled by the army, but I was stunned by how quickly ordinary people who so recently had seemed to support the Islamists and their vision for Egypt's future could turn against them. "Brotherhood" had become a catch-all term synonymous with everything to be hated and feared by its opposite, "honorable citizens." Xenophobic fear of "foreign hands" in general and hatred of pro-Brotherhood

Qatar and its television channel Al Jazeera in particular, was rife. At the same time, Brotherhood supporters were exaggerating their plight online, claiming that six thousand people had died at Rabaa and that military planes had bombed survivors, calling for bloody revenge against the regime and those—particularly Christians—who supported it.

The number of formally affiliated Muslim Brothers in Egypt was relatively small—estimates ranged from 300,000 to 1 million[11]—but suspicion stretched far beyond the organization's official members. Making the "Rabaa sign"—a hand with four fingers held aloft, as "Rabaa" means "fourth" in Arabic—was now sufficient grounds for arrest and detention, as was sharing the sign on social media. Even using the phrase "military coup" was enough to mark you as "Brotherhood," ripe for reporting by neighbors or colleagues to the police hotlines trailed on nightly news programs, because honorable citizens referred to "the June 30 revolution." When I traveled round the city, I saw boiler-suited public workers tirelessly whitewashing over the graffiti that sprang up each night—"Sisi is a killer" or simply "Sisi" with a star of David—meaning "Sisi is a Zionist agent."

Everyone was on edge. The hysteria had exhausted many people I knew, even those who'd been most active in the revolution against Mubarak. Ayman and Abu el-Hassan were repeating the mantra of the burned-out, "I can't think about politics anymore." Mazen was still lying low, in shock from the death of his friends at Rabaa. Amr was more cynical than ever, his long dark eyes bitter.

"They're naive," he said scornfully of the small band of liberal activists trying to steer a course between the army and the Brotherhood, the same people he'd once marched with in

Tahrir. He himself was deep in paperwork, focused on the emigration to Canada he'd planned in 2010. He could see no happy outcome to this asymmetrical tussle between the army and the Islamists.

I'd caught their unease. The illusion of safety I'd felt from being a Westerner in Egypt was long gone. Children and adults shouted "foreigner" at me in the street, their faces hostile. As a holder of a foreign press card, I was automatically a subject of suspicion. There were strange clicks and silences on my phone line now, and state security agents called to question my housemates while I was out. My apartment building's *bawab*, who I'd been friendly with for two years, had become edgy and prying, and I suspected he was reporting to them.

In early October, a kitschy anthem called "Teslam el-Ayadi," "Bless Your Hands," blasted from every second car, shop and street corner in Cairo. To a catchy clap-along beat, an array of aging Mubarak-era singers celebrated the "heroes of the crossing"—the surprise attack into Israeli-occupied Sinai that had started the October war of 1973.

Open our history books
And let's tell the world who those people are
May our Christian priest and our Muslim sheikh
Tell the world what '73 means[12]

Despite its lyrics, "Bless Your Hands" had been recorded not for the annual 6th of October public holiday, but to celebrate the summer's military takeover. The myth of glorious victory over Israel in 1973 was the cornerstone of the army's legitimacy. Although the conflict had actually ended via a

UN-brokered cease-fire with Israeli forces poised fewer than a hundred miles from Cairo, in Egyptian minds the success of the initial foray across the Suez Canal was a longed-for reversal of the catastrophic defeat in the Six Day War of 1967. Faith in the army as Egypt's rightful guardians, heavily battered in 1967, was restored. This year, honorable citizens were vowing to mark the holiday by begging the coup leader, General Abdel Fattah el-Sisi, to run for president.

On October 6 itself, Tahrir Square, symbol of the uprising against Mubarak, was firmly in army hands. Tanks blocked the streets around the square and officers manned a single checkpoint entrance with long security lines. I queued with everyone else, remembering the lines to get into Rabaa two months before. Inside, the atmosphere was one of family festivity. Vendors sold balloons, cotton candy and posters of Sisi with Nasser, Sisi with a roaring lion, Sisi with his trademark sunglasses. The military leader, invariably pictured in a snug-fitting uniform and sunglasses, had become an instant icon— an action hero for men, a pinup for middle-aged women.

"Egypt wants to say thank you to the army!" shouted an MC.

"Thank you, thank you to the army!" the crowd roared, transforming into an ecstatic sea of waving Egyptian flags. One man was carrying a portrait of Sisi bedecked with tinsel and Christmas baubles, pausing to kiss the general's picture repeatedly on his resolute military mouth.

"I love Sisi, he saved us from the Brotherhood, from the terrorists!" he said. "He must be our new president!" But like the endless programs celebrating the military I saw on TV, the festivity was underpinned by violence and spite. Another man danced past, thrusting a poster into my hands. When I unrolled it, I found an image of a grinning Sisi preparing to slaughter a sheep with Morsi's head crudely photoshopped onto it.

The next day, I turned on the TV to see news of the scattered violence that had become common since the coup. Two rocket-propelled grenades had hit a satellite station in southern Cairo. A car-bomb attack on a security headquarters in Sinai had killed three policemen. And six army conscripts on patrol in Ismailia, on the Suez Canal, had been shot by masked gunmen.[13] Government supporters blamed "Muslim Brotherhood militias."

That evening, I got a text message from a youth leader of Life Makers I'd met in 2011. Since the coup, he was having to keep a low profile to avoid arrest. "One of the soldiers killed in Ismailia was from Life Makers. Do you want to come on a condolence visit to his family?"

Three days later, I met two young men from Life Makers at the metro station in Dar el-Salaam, a crowded lower-middle-class Cairo neighborhood of mud-brick apartment buildings. As we walked further from the station, the streets became narrower and muddier. Tuk-tuks swerved around us, decorated with ultraviolet lights or axle blades like Persian war chariots, pumping *mahraganat* music, the teenage drivers shouting to each other. It was Thursday night, the end of the last working day before the long Eid al-Adha holiday, and the crowds on the streets were happy and relaxed.

We picked our way through the market street, passing vegetable stalls, barbershops, groceries, household-goods stores, butchers, haberdashers, TV repair shops and stalls selling women's underwear, hairbrushes, socks, plugs and electrical fuses. Street corners were marked by a rash of the ubiquitous Sisi posters, including one of him adding Morsi's severed head to a cauldron in which other Muslim Brothers were already boiling.

Inside the family's modest apartment, the one living space was lined with new stacking chairs they had rented to receive mourners, the blue velour upholstery harshly bright against the faded walls. We were greeted by the soldier's brother Ahmed and his father, Mohamed, a heavily bearded middle-aged man in a gray robe and prayer cap, who didn't shake my hand but politely placed his own over his heart. He and his sons were well-known local Brotherhood figures.

"Moez was twenty-three. He had memorized the entire Quran, he was an imam, he gave the Friday sermons," he began, gesturing us toward the blue chairs and sitting down heavily himself. "He only had two months of his military service left." Military service was widely dreaded and for Muslim Brothers there was an additional difficulty. They had been banned from the army until the 2011 revolution, and anti-Islamist feeling lingered.

"Moez joined under Morsi, and there were many other Brothers in the army, so we thought he would be OK," Mohamed continued. "But at 1 p.m. on Monday, an officer called and just told me, 'Your son Moez is dead.' I didn't believe him. Moez had just called me the day before, on October 6, to see if there were any protests near our house and if we were OK."

The call to prayer filtered through from the street outside and Mohamed excused himself. His shoulders slumped as he walked. When he had left the room, his son Ahmed sighed.

"OK, I'm a free man now," he said. "I'll tell you what happened." He started to talk in a low, urgent voice. "After the coup, because everyone knew Moez was Brotherhood, things started to get difficult for him in the army. The officers knew, and some of them became hostile.

"He came home last Thursday, because we were preparing for his engagement party, which should have been today. That day he told me that one Brother in the army, an opponent of Sisi, spoke to the officers about some orders he disagreed with and they stripped him, beat him and tied him to a flagpost.

"So at 1 p.m. on Monday they called and said you have to come and collect the body, we don't have an ambulance for it. We drove to the military hospital in Ismailia, to wash Moez's body. My father had begged them, 'Please don't do this, we want to do it ourselves.'" According to Islam, the dead person should be washed by relatives of the same sex, and buried as soon as possible.

"Here—do you want to see a picture of Moez?" He swiped at his tablet, and called up two photos. The first image was a dark-eyed young man in a sky-blue polo shirt with a navy collar, his expression calm and cheerful. The second, slightly blurred as if the camera had been shaking, showed his corpse from the abdomen up, covered in abrasions and dark marks. His face, though bruised and swollen, was still recognizable. Ahmed's eyes filled with tears.

"That's my little brother," he said. One of the men from Life Makers leaned across and gripped his hand. These before-and-after photos of young men and women, alive and smiling, then dead and disfigured, had become sadly familiar since the first and most famous, of Khaled Said. Arabic-language media had far fewer taboos about showing graphic images of the victims of violence, and people I knew often shared pictures of mangled corpses.

"Do you know what happened?" I asked.

"They gave us the official story," Ahmed said. "He was sent on patrol with five other soldiers in a military jeep. Somewhere outside the base in Ismailia, an unmarked car opened fire on them, and they were all shot and killed. By terrorists, Islamists.

"But when we were washing his body, we found that his legs were broken. He had long knife cuts on his arms and a stab wound in his neck. I asked the officer how he explained this, and we didn't get a proper answer. He said that after the terrorists shot them, they came to the car and stabbed them, to make sure they were dead. But this doesn't make sense. How could they, when they were so near the army base? And why would they—if they wanted to make sure they were dead, wouldn't they just shoot them again?

"A high-up army officer called my father yesterday. He said, 'Why have you and your son been talking to people about this? We told you what happened, now stop saying there is another story.' But we won't stop. We want the Egyptian people to think, to use logic. Not just about what happened to Moez, but about everything that is happening in Egypt these days."

"What do you think the real story is?" I asked.

"We don't know," he said, "but we think because Moez was Muslim Brotherhood, and most Brothers were fasting on this day, an officer collected them all in one car and did something with them. We don't know."

"What did the other families think?"

Ahmed shrugged. "The other families didn't ask the army if they could wash their sons' bodies, so they never saw them or what wounds they had. The army had already shrouded them." He flicked back to the first photo of his brother, and looked at his smile. "Moez had just finished studying at al-Azhar, to be an imam, and he had to do this military service before getting a job. He was volunteering with illiterate people, there are so many in this neighborhood. Believe me, Moez was an angel." He began to cry quietly.

His father shuffled back into the room and sat alone on a chair against the far wall. The younger men got up to pray, spreading a bedspread for a prayer carpet, standing shoulder to shoulder behind Ahmed, who recited the call to prayer in a trained voice still hoarse from crying. While they bowed and knelt, his father shuffled his cracked bare feet in his slippers and stared unseeingly at his mobile phone. I could feel the sadness spreading from him.

When we left, we passed the rest of the chairs they had hired, stacked in the muddy street outside. None of us knew what had happened to Moez in the jeep outside Ismailia, and it was unlikely his family would ever find out. The fact that they suspected the military of killing him for his political affiliations showed how splintered the country had become. While his fellow citizens were dancing and celebrating the army in Tahrir, a healthy young man could too easily end up dead—killed somehow in the ugly wrangle over Egypt's future.

By November, street protests without police approval were banned. After the anti-Morsi demonstrations of June 30 and the marches of July 26, when Sisi had urged the people to "take to the streets and . . . give me, the army and the police, a mandate to confront possible terrorism," the regime had no more use for them. As the winter wore on, the curfew was lifted but anti-Brotherhood hysteria escalated. Now the TV news showed Morsi, seen in public for the first time since the coup, in the defendants' cage of a Cairo courtroom, charged with ordering the killing of protesters during his time in office. Whenever I took a taxi over the Nile I passed people standing on the bridges holding placards asking drivers to "honk for the death penalty for the Brotherhood." A white stork was detained by police as a suspected spy after a fisherman saw in its feathers a "suspicious device"—which turned out to be a conservation tag attached by French scientists. State security questioned Vodafone over a TV advert starring a puppet called Abla Fahita, which was thought to be sending coded messages about bombings to the Brotherhood.

Qatar, where several senior Brothers had sought refuge, and its Al Jazeera satellite news channel were at the heart of the paranoia, suspected of plotting to destabilize the Egyptian state. Three Al Jazeera journalists, two with Western passports, were seized from the Marriott hotel in Cairo, and footage of their arrest was broadcast on a pro-army satellite channel to a soundtrack of menacing music from the Hollywood film *Thor*. In December, the Brotherhood was legally designated a terrorist organization.

In this tide of repression, universities had become an island of dissent. Whereas the slightly older generation who had led the protests against Mubarak had been exhausted by the previous two years, the students were younger, fresher, faster and fueled by the recent outrage of Rabaa. The center of the resistance was the Islamic al-Azhar University in Cairo, which Sara attended, and whose 120,000 students were overwhelmingly sympathetic to the Brotherhood and Morsi. Students Against the Coup, an inter-university umbrella movement formed at Rabaa, helped coordinate protests, arranging more than two hundred demonstrations a month across twenty-four campuses since the start of the academic year in September.[14]

A regime crackdown was inevitable. On-campus protests were criminalized, and security forces were given free run of university campuses, reversing a 2009 ruling that had kept them outside the gates. Tear-gassings, beatings and arrests inside universities became common; fourteen students were shot dead, hundreds arrested and scores expelled.

The state-appointed university administrators cooperated with the government. But their students were another matter. January 2014 was exam season in Egypt and at al-Azhar the students who were protesting for Rabaa went on strike. On the female campus, Sara went to her first exam and scrawled across the covering sheet: "I am against the military coup and I will never answer this exam while my brothers are under the ground and my sisters are behind bars." Then she stood up and tore the exam paper in half.

"What do you think you're doing?" shouted the lecturer who was invigilating.

Sara stood up straighter. "I can't bear to sit here and answer your exam questions while our fellow students are sitting in prison, right now. I'm not selfish like you." Tears of anger ran down her face, and her close friends began to cry in sympathy.

The lecturer called campus security. Instead of running, Sara stayed, clinging to her desk so they couldn't drag her away, shouting "Down with military rule!" It was the slogan from the Mohamed Mahmoud protests of November 2011, when the military council was in power.

"We're not going to let you go this time," the head of security told Sara when she arrived. "You're coming downstairs with me now." Sara understood the threat. Outside the campus gates, the police waited, ready to take her for detention, beating and worse. Human rights groups had identified a "general politicization of sexual violence, aimed both at stamping out revolt and demonizing the opposition"— directed at both Islamists and liberals, men and women.[15] As well as serving as a direct punishment to women who dared protest, the attacks were designed to humiliate the men close to them, showing that they were unable to protect them and therefore less than the "real men" in the army and police. On top of that, the corrupt justice system made most victims unwilling to file complaints against police officers, soldiers and prison guards.

But Sara was still not afraid. "Look what they're doing," she shouted to her classmates, clinging even harder to her desk. "They're handing me over to the police. Why?" She turned back to the head of security and the lecturer, who hovered uncertainly, their expressions sheepish, before her. "You've sold your consciences, both of you! You should be responsible for educating and protecting us. Instead you're delivering us to be beaten and tortured in the regime's jails!" By now, the exam hall was in uproar. All thirty girls were crying loudly, their exam long forgotten.

"Give her ID card back and just let her out," the lecturer told the head of security in an undertone, horrified by the public scene. This time, Sara escaped.

Later that month, I met her in a pastry shop close to the university. To me, middle-class Egyptian girls, especially those brought up in devout Muslim families, seemed so much younger and more innocent than their university-aged counterparts in the UK. They couldn't travel alone, live alone or have serious relationships—let alone drink, smoke, wear clothes that weren't extremely conservative or in many cases even makeup. They were raised to be demure, modest and to defer to men. But when conversations turned to their political and religious convictions, I was amazed by the inner steeliness of these gentle-mannered girls. Sara was the same. She was petite and pretty in a flowered headscarf, quick to giggle, but when she spoke about the military coup and those who supported it, her voice turned icy.

"People in Egypt are like slaves," she said. "They want a pharaoh to worship. They can't bear to be free. When I was in the exam hall, striking, I told the lecturer, 'We're fighting for your freedom too.' She told me, 'I'm OK with this situation, I don't want your freedom.'" She raised her eyebrows scornfully. "They are weak, and afraid."

"You don't feel afraid?" When I now came face-to-face with the security force's black trucks with their masked, black-clad, gun-carrying soldiers, I was afraid of them. I was afraid of state security agents turning up at my door, I was afraid of ending up in an Egyptian prison, and I was afraid of "honorable citizens" and being beaten on the street as a spy— all of which had happened to foreigners and journalists. And I was older, more experienced and, with my Western passport and government press card, far less vulnerable than Sara.

She shook her head. "My story, of losing my fiancé, Karim, in Rabaa, is one of thousands. Too many of my girlfriends lost husbands or fiancés or brothers, dead or imprisoned. And these experiences made us very strong." Her voice turned even colder. "We have experienced everything. We have experienced blood. We have experienced death and being detained. We have lost everything, our lives, our beloveds' lives. So nothing is going to bend us anymore. We are going to continue on our way. Because there is no other solution. Either we are going to live free in this country, or we are going to paradise."

I remembered her account of the bodies surrounding her in the mosque at Rabaa. For Sara "going to paradise" was not a figure of speech.

"And you're starting with your university?" I asked.

Her hard expression melted into a smile. "History teaches us that because of our Islamist background, the revolution always starts in al-Azhar," she said proudly. "Suleiman el-Halabi, who killed the leader of the French occupation, was an al-Azhar student. So we have this long tradition." She laughed. I knew the story of Suleiman el-Halabi and I thought he was a gruesome role model. In 1800, two years after Napoleon invaded Egypt, the twenty-three-year-old Syrian Kurdish student had stabbed the general's deputy to death. The French authorities tortured him by burning his hand to the bone, then executed him by impaling him on a sharpened stake.

"Aren't your parents ever worried about you?" I asked. "They always let you protest?"

"Many friends' parents stopped them," she said. "But my parents believe no one dies before their time. They have a very Islamist background. They believe this life, this world, is a jihad." Like martyrdom, I'd become used to hearing devout believers talk about jihad, which meant, simply, any kind of effort to please God. "So I keep telling my father that as he wants us to live well, with dignity, he has to want us to die well, with dignity," she continued, her spine straightening and her face glowing with certainty. "And there is no more honorable death than being killed for your country, your cause and your dreams."

I noticed that though the regime painted their Islamist opponents as religious fanatics ready to wreak violence on Egypt's women and children, she didn't say "being killed for your religion." The slight young woman sitting in front of me loved her country. She was young, educated and should have been looking forward to a bright future, but her experiences had left her so embittered that she was ready to lay down her life in the fight against the regime. She may have been part of a minority, but I couldn't imagine how Sisi could preside over a peaceful Egypt when a young woman like this regarded him with such absolute hatred.

Suddenly, Sara's eyes filled with tears. She looked less like a freedom fighter than like a sad young girl.

"I keep asking myself why I wasn't killed with Karim in the square," she said. "But I believe I still have work to do, so I stay here."

While the students protested, the rest of the country was preparing for a referendum. Ostensibly on a new constitution drafted after Morsi's removal, it was widely seen as a vote on Sisi's expected presidential candidacy. The irony of validating a military coup through the ballot box was not lost on Sisi's opponents, who organized small street protests, though protesting was now illegal and police were poised to detain and abuse anyone who even looked like an Islamist. On the first day of the referendum, Ruqayah was captured near al-Azhar University as she tried to reach a protest. Together with two thirteen-year-old girls, her little sister and a friend, she had just passed the KFC where students gathered for snacks after class when she saw black-clad security soldiers chasing two teenage girls in veils and long skirts. They caught one of them and began to twist her to the ground.

"Let her go, you animals," screamed the thirteen-year-olds, running forward. Ruqayah chased after them. The girl scrambled to her feet and ran, and the police seized the thirteen-year-olds instead. Suddenly, Ruqayah found her own head in a vice-like lock under a man's arm. She could smell his sweat as he dragged her roughly to the police van.

At the district police station they threw the girls into a windowless room. There were six boys already in there, sitting in a row on the floor, blindfolded with their own clothes. Whispering to them, they found out that they were also from al-Azhar schools. Ruqayah, at fifteen, was the oldest of them all. Two of the boys were taken next door and beaten for laughing together. Another boy asked to go to the toilet.

"We're not in a nursery now," the policeman guarding them said in a bored voice.

"Please. I'm sick," the boy said. His voice was weak and Ruqayah could see that under his blindfold his face was ashen.

"If you want to die, go ahead and die."

Ruqayah thought the police might have mercy on them when they realized how old they were, but it only made it worse. An officer came in to have a look at them.

"Your parents haven't done a good job, so now we're going to bring you up properly," he told them. "We'll make sure you're well behaved before you leave."

At nightfall, the policemen took Ruqayah, her sister and friend down to the communal women's cell under the police station. Below ground, there was a heavy smell of unwashed bodies. At the gate of the cell was one of the women prisoners, tasked with searching new admissions.

"Search these ones," the police told her. "And do it properly."

The woman looked at the girls, veiled and modestly dressed in their drab Islamist clothes, and grinned. While the police looked on, she shoved her hands under the girls' veils, down their fronts and between their legs. Two of the girls were wearing sanitary towels.

"What's this, then?" she asked them, raising her rough voice to make a show for the police.

"We have our periods," they whispered, feeling like they were about to die of humiliation. The police laughed.

"Oh I'm not sure about that," the woman said loudly. "We'll have to check." As she stripped them, Ruqayah gritted her teeth and prayed for protection for her little sister.

It was almost a relief when they were finally thrust into the cell. Though it was January, the coldest month of the year, it was unbearably hot and airless. Thirty adult women were packed together in the tiny room, and most of them were smoking. Ruqayah looked around at the faces turned toward her. *Oh God, please protect us,* she thought. *They are all criminals, not political prisoners. Who knows what they've done— drugs, prostitution, murdered people?* She had seen people killed in front of her, but she had never been close to a criminal before. The women stared back at the girls, taking in their neat clothes and frightened faces.

"Your dirty friends who died at Rabaa went straight to hell." They followed it with a cacophony of obscenities.

Ruqayah's sister and her friend finally started to cry. Before today, they had hardly heard a curse word in their lives. They huddled together, holding hands, as the hours passed. Eventually, the women grew bored and left them alone.

In the middle of the night, a policeman took Ruqayah upstairs for interrogation.

"You support Morsi and the terrorist Brotherhood," the officer said to her, leaning back behind his desk.

"Yes, I do," she replied. She felt tiny, perched on the chair opposite him.

"And this mobile phone with the pro-Brotherhood pictures on it belongs to you."

"Yes, it does."

He exhaled cigarette smoke over her head. "You know this cell you and the other girls are in now? Do you like it? You could all be in a place like this for the next five years. Or more. Easily."

Ruqayah was silent.

"OK, if you don't want to talk, let's look at the list of charges. Attempting to take pictures of a military building. Attempting to obstruct the referendum process. Participating in the illegal al-Azhar University protests. Membership of a banned terrorist organization. That means the Muslim Brotherhood," he added.

Ruqayah had to protest. "We're not members. We just hate injustice."

Bored, the officer sent her back to the cell. After two days, the girls were released without charge. They knew they were the lucky ones—they had heard all the stories about torture and rape in the police stations and prisons. The uprising against Mubarak had been sparked by the brutality of poorly trained and unaccountable police. Three years later, little had changed. The police were back on the streets and citizens were still at their mercy.

A few days later, Ruqayah heard the referendum results on the radio—a 98% "yes" vote for Sisi's constitution. It was like the Mubarak-era referendums her parents told her about, when the president would return triumphantly to office with more than 90% of the vote each time.

For the moment, not even the most ridiculous propaganda an authoritarian state could dream up could dent Sisi's popularity. In February 2014, army doctors announced they could detect and cure both AIDS and hepatitis C—of which Egypt had the highest infection rate in the world—with handheld devices that looked like a television antenna attached to a plastic handle. More bizarre still were the claims made by the skull-faced general in charge of the research.

"I take AIDs from the patient and feed the patient on AIDs, I give it to him as a kofta skewer to feed on," he said. "I take the disease, and I give it to him as food, and this is the top of scientific miracles."[16]

Respectable Egyptian scientists were aghast. It seemed further proof that the army lived, North Korea–style, in a parallel reality of its own devising, firmly insulated from the outside world. Soon afterward Sisi announced he was resigning from the army in order to run for the presidency. Artful billboards and placards sprang up around Egypt, showing him not in his familiar uniform but in a tracksuit, polo shirt or smart suit, with a discreet prayer bruise, calculated to set housewives' hearts aflutter.

Whereas the fall of Mubarak had brought Egyptians— liberals, Islamists, young and old—together at least temporarily, the return of the army had now succeeded in setting them deeply against each other. Hatred, fear and suspicion reigned, the Islamist enemy the army had manufactured once again justifying all its excesses of repression.

But while setting the people against each other with one hand, the regime was manufacturing an unconvincing image of unity and optimism with the other. When I passed through it now, Rabaa looked like any other of Cairo's clogged traffic intersections, though its rebuilt mosque was too pristinely whitewashed for a city coated in dust and pollution. A billboard announced the ongoing "beautification and development of Rabaa" and a brand-new sculpture of two crooked arms holding a marble ball, swathed in plastic netting, rose amid the traffic. The military engineers who erected it had explained that the large arm was the army, the smaller the police, and between them they held the Egyptian people. Instead of "Bless Your Hands," the clunky, old-fashioned anthem to past military victories, every street corner now blasted a song called "Boshrat Kheir," "Good Omen." The video, based on Pharrell Williams's worldwide hit "Happy," showed smiling Egyptians of all ages and sizes, from everywhere across the country, dancing and holding up signs with their city's name. Set to an infuriating, mind-numbing, addictive dance beat, "Good Omen" was a slick modern harbinger of Egypt's bright future under Sisi:

You're writing tomorrow on your own terms
That's a good omen.[17]

7

Amr, Amal and Mazen:
Survival Lessons

On the night of Sisi's inauguration in June 2014, Cairo was overtaken by wild celebrations. Cars careened through the streets sounding their horns, trailing Egyptian flags, girls leaning from the windows screaming in excitement. "Good Omen" blared from millions of stereos, and ecstatic crowds packed Tahrir, supervised by the army, unconcerned by the fact that once again the power kept going out because of chronic electricity shortages. I wondered at how short people's memories seemed, and how fickle their allegiances. Fireworks were exploding at crazy angles from balconies and street corners as they had in February 2011 when Mubarak stepped down, in June 2012 when Morsi was elected and in July 2013 when he was removed by the army.

I was sitting in Cairo's biggest mall with Amr, drinking tea and sheltering from the heat and noise outside. He was uncharacteristically glum, rolling his eyes about the Sisi-mania outside. Amr had given up on activism long before, but friends and acquaintances still followed his mordant dissections of Egyptian politics and history on Facebook. They called him *el bouma*, the owl—a nickname that wasn't affectionate so much as half-wary, half-respectful, because the owl was a bird of very bad omen.

Amr pretended not to mind. "We'll see who's an owl when they're all eating each other in ten years' time," he said. But I could see that he did.

Now the power had failed in the mall, the air conditioning was out and greasy gray smoke from the food-court kitchens was rolling down the corridors. The generators powered only dim, haphazard strips of lighting. Amr looked around disbelievingly at the crowds with their bulging shopping bags.

"We're in one of the most privileged places in the country, the castle of the upper middle classes," he said. "And they can't keep the power on. But people are still shopping away, happy about Sisi. This country is falling to bits and they don't think it will affect them."

On my way home, I passed Tahrir and saw the fireworks exploding over it. But I didn't stop, partly because I felt so downcast to see Egyptians celebrating another military officer elected with more than 96% of the vote—and partly because Sisi's supporters, now, were encouraged to hate foreigners.

The people I knew who had greeted Mubarak's overthrow in Tahrir were also missing from the square. Amr wasn't there, and neither were the bloggers and human rights activists he had celebrated with nearly three and a half years earlier. With Sisi's election, it was clear that the revolution as they had dreamed of it had failed. The returning military state had cracked down hard on the best-known activists of 2011. Some were dead; some in prison; others, like the We Are All Khaled Said administrator Wael Ghonim, had been forced abroad.

Mazen wasn't there, and neither were the moderate young Islamists he had marched with against Mubarak. Some had died at Rabaa, others were in prison for protesting or supporting the Muslim Brotherhood, and the rest lay low at home, their hearts full of hate for Sisi and the state.

Amal, who had gathered petitions for Morsi's removal and marched against him on June 30, wasn't there either. The fall of the Brotherhood hadn't brought the liberation from authoritarian rule she was hoping for. She was horrified when three youth leaders who had campaigned against Mubarak, the army and Morsi alike were imprisoned for allegedly assaulting police officers. The regime was turning on the very people who had—inadvertently—paved its way to power.

Sara and Ruqayah and the students weren't there. The girls had gone underground—"They've left the movement," Youssof, a student activist who knew them eventually said— and knowing the dangers to them I didn't want to try too hard to find them. Footage of Youssof had been produced as "evidence" in the trial of other activists, and I didn't understand how he had escaped jail himself. Rights groups estimated thirteen hundred students had been imprisoned since September for protesting against the regime, many of them seized from their campuses and dorms.[1] The government itself admitted that twenty-two thousand people had been arrested on political grounds over the past year; an independent NGO that monitored political arrests put the figure at forty-one thousand.[2]

When I woke up the next morning, a video from Tahrir was circulating online. In the midst of the celebrations, a woman had been surrounded by a mob who ripped her clothes off and sexually assaulted her, then poured boiling water over her. The blurry mobile phone footage showed glimpses of her blood-spattered naked body as she was finally grappled from the crowd and bundled into an ambulance. It was part of an epidemic of sexual violence against women around the square that had escalated since 2011. On the day Sisi had announced Morsi's removal, rights groups recorded eighty mob assaults and rapes of women in Tahrir.[3] The attacks were organized and systematic, though no one could identify who was behind them. But their effect was clear—to punish women for voicing their political opinions on the street, just as they could be punished with assault and rape once they were arrested. Three days later, the new president was photographed at the victim's hospital bedside, stiffly proffering a bunch of red roses.

An atmosphere of threat had seeped into the city, and crowds no longer felt safe for those who stood out among them. A couple of weeks before Sisi's inauguration, my flatmate Maggie and I had gone to the *moulid* of Sayyida Zeinab, an annual multiday festival honoring the granddaughter of the Prophet that, the year before, we had visited with Abu el-Hassan.

No one knew whether Sayyida Zeinab was really buried in her shrine in central Cairo—Shia Muslims claimed she lay under a pure gold dome in Damascus—but it had been a place of pilgrimage for centuries. People called her El Sitt, The Lady, and believed her intercession could make women fertile and heal the sick. Every day, traffic and a steady stream of worshippers swirled around the latest iteration of the saint's mosque, a graceless nineteenth-century imitation of Cairo's medieval masterpieces. Her tomb was enclosed in an ornate cross-latticed silver cage under a high dome in a chamber divided by an eight-foot-high screen that separated women from men. Normally, it was a subdued place, the mosque attendants shepherding women into the cramped, grimy space set aside for them, to cling to the bars as they muttered prayers and petitions.

But one night during the *moulid* of summer 2013, Maggie, Abu el-Hassan and I had gone to the shrine and found it transformed. The grim-faced attendants were nowhere to be seen and women and families had gathered in the spacious section usually reserved for men. Forty white-robed men from Upper Egypt sat in the antechamber singing an ode to the Prophet in resonant voices. Women clutched at the bars of the tomb and shrieked "*Ya Sitt!*" "Oh Lady!" tears running down their faces. A man brought his elderly mother, who had survived an operation; young mothers brought babies; ragged homeless men sat along the walls and families from the Ahmadiyya sect, religious refugees from Pakistan, came in their distinctive clothes. Long past midnight, men carried in a stepladder and rough plastic sacks, and climbed up to garland the top of the tomb with red roses and bunches of fresh mint. Others picked their way through the crowd sitting cross-legged in groups on the carpet, handing out sweets and tea and extra bundles of the mint. We sat while everyone sang and prayed until the tiny stained-glass windows set into the dome high above grew bright.

To me, that night at Sayyida Zeinab's shrine seemed beautiful, a respite from the exhausting social judgments and class divisions that governed life in Egypt, and I wanted to experience it again. Outside the shrine, *moulid*s could be rowdy and women were often harassed, so we had arrived in the late afternoon when the streets were full of families, swathed ourselves in dark baggy clothes and headscarves, and brought a male friend as backup. We watched the old men from Upper Egypt in robes and turbans dancing traditional stick dances, a magic show with a ventriloquist and a levitating girl, and women handing out roses and sweets. It was the friendly, fun-loving Egypt of the "Good Omen" video.

But this year when we went to the shrine, Maggie and I were turned away brusquely from the main door. As we walked the few yards to the women's side entrance, groups of men loitering around the mosque turned, in an instant, into a mob. We were groped and mauled by a hundred hands, shoved and dragged before we barely managed to fight our way into the women's enclosure, a small sunken courtyard surrounded by tall railings. When we turned back, scores of men were clinging to the metal bars. They were shouting about whores and spies and "foreign hands"—the catch-all term for the enemy agents state TV constantly inveighed against—in the logicless howl of a lynch mob. A single teenage police conscript in an ill-fitting uniform stood looking at us with helpless hostility. He was scared, too, because there was nothing preventing the crowd from surging through the gateway except the last shreds of taboo.

That night, we were lucky. Eventually, we were dragged out of the enclosure by six undercover state security officers who had been pretending to sell mobile phone accessories outside the mosque. As the crowd flinched away at the sight of them, the officers hauled us up the street and shoved us into a passing taxi. "Good Omen" was playing on the radio and the driver was cheerfully singing along. Maggie and I looked at each other, our hearts beating hard and our clothes drenched with the sweat of the mob. When we arrived home our street was swallowed up in the darkness of a power cut. Only our apartment building was illuminated, because the landlord had used a *wasta*—a corrupt connection—to tap into an alternate power supply. The *bawab*s were sitting in front of the building in the dark, smoking and listening to "Good Omen" playing tinnily on an old mobile.

"You were asking to be raped," shrugged pro-army acquaintances who found out what had happened. "Thank God the police saved you." But it was hard to feel grateful to the state for rescuing us from a hatred it had incited. And intolerance of those who stood out wasn't the price of greater freedom for the majority of Egyptians. Attacks against women, the jailing of dissidents and xenophobia were all symptoms of a public space that was shrinking further into ideological, racial and religious uniformity.

Despite the celebrations over the election of a military man who depicted himself as Egypt's only source of security, the country was increasingly driven by fear. The state's existential battle with "terrorism"—whether it manifested as bomb-building jihadis or badge-wearing students—was coming to control every aspect of daily life. Tanks, APCs and riot police trucks sat at Tahrir Square and other former protest locations, black-clad conscripts lounging in bored groups or fetching bags of takeaway food for the officers. Even trivial civil infractions met with a theatrical display of force. When Sisi ordered the removal of the street vendors who had colonized downtown Cairo since 2011, obstructing traffic with tables of cheap Chinese-made clothes and toys, gun-toting commandos in black balaclavas and ski goggles were posted every twenty paces along main streets to prevent their return.

There were a few stubborn pockets of resistance. Every Friday small Islamist marches turned out, in defiance of the protest law, in densely populated working-class areas of north Cairo like Matareyya, Ain Shams and Abu Zaabal, where Abu el-Hassan lived. The police sometimes ignored them, sometimes dispersed them with arbitrary violence, tear-gassing everyone and shooting two or three protesters dead each time. Brotherhood-linked accounts shared photos of the "martyrs" on Twitter and Facebook and called for the overthrow of the regime, and life carried on.

In the universities, the students continued their protests. I enjoyed talking to them, because their optimism was refreshing after older activists' grim resignation and the Brotherhood's nihilistic talk of martyrdom. They still laughed off tear gas, beatings and imprisonment, and they used words—like "revolution"—I rarely heard spoken in sincerity anymore. Now there was a stark difference between them and the people ten or twelve years older who had struggled against the regime in the 2000s and led the demonstrations against Mubarak. But despite the students' cheerfulness, I had doubts about the staying power of even those who claimed divine motivation. Surely they would burn out like their elders?

Elsewhere, as if to fulfill the regime's doom-laden warnings, terrorist attacks continued. In Sinai the jihadis of Ansar Beit el-Maqdis were escalating their campaign of violence, beheading locals they accused of collaborating with the state or Israel, and launching increasingly sophisticated and effective assaults on military and police outposts. In a single attack in October, they killed thirty-three soldiers with car bombs and heavy weaponry. The next month, the group pledged allegiance to Abu Bakr al-Baghdadi and declared itself an outpost of Islamic State in Egypt, taking the new name Sinai Province.

As the fierce heat of the year dispersed, Amal asked Maggie and me for a strange favor—to model bellydance costumes for her. She had fallen in love with dance in Beijing, where she had first had the freedom to take lessons. Now she had started teaching dance herself after work and at weekends, had set up a little studio in her Cairo apartment; and was starting a business creating the elaborate costumes with her youngest sister. It was another act of rebellion. As society became more conservative, attitudes had turned sharply against the art of *raqs sharqi*, oriental dance, and the dancers who worked in the big hotels and on the Nile cruise boats were now mainly South American or east European. It was hard for Amal to find Egyptian girls who'd be photographed wearing the tight revealing costumes— and anyway, foreign models made sales more likely. I hesitated— the photos could ruin my relationships with conservative contacts—but I liked Amal and wanted to help her. And these days there weren't enough opportunities for fun.

In Amal's bedroom, Maggie and I were safety-pinned into lurid scraps of spandex fringed with gold coins and beadwork, our faces plastered into unrecognizability by a makeup artist friend of Amal's. Neither of us knew oriental dance and we posed stiffly with the tambourines and gold canes dancers used as props while Amal, giggling helplessly, tried to direct us.

"My hips don't move that way. I think I'm missing some joints," Maggie complained as Amal demonstrated a seductive shimmy.

"You English girls just haven't got it," the trendy young photographer kept saying, grimacing through the viewfinder at a wooden tableau where we pretended to play the same tambourine.

"How's this?" I asked Maggie, draping myself faux-suggestively backward to show off the next costume. The thick makeup caked in the creases round my eyes and the bright orange fabric clashed horribly with my pale skin. Maggie, in red Lycra straps that crisscrossed up her arms, blinking under the weight of huge false eyelashes, didn't look much better.

Afterward, sore from laughing and relieved to be back in jeans, we chatted with Amal as she held her baby daughter on her lap. The year before, we had been invited to her wedding to an Irish teacher. Amal's relatives had come up from the Fayoum in their dignified country clothes, and the Irish family arrived in leather jackets. They were unable to say a word to each other, but everyone had danced together happily enough.

Now Amal turned over the dance costumes she had patiently sewn. Each would sell for hundreds of dollars.

"The idea of a woman being financially independent scares most people here," she said. "It's like saying, 'I don't need men anymore,' which is like—*what??!*" Her voice rose in pantomimed horror and her baby wriggled uneasily. "You know, I was raised to believe that I have to be dependent on a man. That's how almost all the women I know are still living. Look at my middle sister."

Having seen the results of Amal's rebellion, her sister had resolved to be her opposite. She had started wearing a face veil and black gloves and socks to hide every inch of her skin. She read the Quran constantly. If the family started watching a movie, she would run out of the room in protest. The dance costumes would fill her with as much horror as the idea of living alone and refusing to wear a headscarf.

"Why do you think you changed your thinking, Amal?" I asked. "So many women don't."

Amal shrugged. "Everyone falls into line. Unless you're exposed to a different culture, which very few people are, or unless you start carving your own way, learning and reading and wanting to be independent and working toward it. Hardly anyone can accept the cost of doing that. And it's a massive turn-off for men here, anyway." She bounced her daughter on her lap, thinking. "They only want to marry someone who never left home, who's happy to stay in, cook, clean and do their laundry, and raise the children. Basically, someone exactly like their mum."

Maggie caught my eye. I knew she was remembering how even the most open-minded of the unmarried men we knew admitted that they were likely to marry only a "nice" girl. Amal looked at us and laughed. She could tell what we were thinking, too.

"Yes, that's why I had to go for a foreign guy. Not that they don't have their own issues . . ."

"Don't worry, we know!" said Maggie.

"But he didn't judge me in the same way. He was willing to accept me as an equal."

"Do you think things can change for women? Will they have more freedom?" I asked.

Amal hesitated. "I thought for a while they might, in 2011," she said. "But now I don't know. Maybe for individuals. But all this stupid stuff, obsessing about sex, about covering women's hair, is because of the vacuum we live in. The economy is so bad, there's unemployment—people don't have anything better to think about. We'll only see a real change if we get a real government, an independent one—I don't count the Brotherhood or the army. And I don't think Israel and the United States will ever allow that."

"I'm guessing you may not stay around to see if that happens," I said. I felt downcast at the possibility of Amal leaving Egypt. I found her courage inspiring and I thought she might inspire other young women too—or at least show them that a different way of living was possible. But Amal could not afford to be sentimental or idealistic. She was driven by the same tough pragmatism that had propelled her out of the Fayoum. She laughed and shook her head. "No way. We may go to Abu Dhabi, or to Ireland," she said. "Or maybe to China again, depending on what jobs we get." She looked down at her daughter, thinking of her future. "But we're not staying here."

To Amr, Egypt's future also looked bleak. He lingered with relish on some favorite ghoulish scenarios.

"Say the government did something stupid to annoy the Israelis," he speculated while I listened in horror. "They could bomb the Aswan dam very easily, and the whole of the Nile Valley would be drowned. Or an epidemic—Ebola maybe, or bubonic plague—with all our overcrowding and the terrible medical facilities, that would wipe 90% of us out too." He paused to think. "Actually, the most likely thing is that food and water will just run out. People are having more and more children. Like I said to you the night Sisi was elected, they'll just end up eating each other in the streets." He was half-serious, but the state had just announced that 2013 had been a year of record population growth and it clearly had no way to feed, educate, house or employ the estimated 116 million people it would be responsible for by 2030.[4]

A few of Amr's old activist friends were still trying to change the course of this future, dashing themselves to pieces against the state. The Islamists had seen the full cost of defiance at Rabaa. Now, liberal activists were ending up in the regime's jails alongside them, living martyrs to the revolution. Some wrote beautiful, inspiring letters from their cells, and their friends and foreign journalists tweeted the most moving passages. But the longer things went on, the less effective these gestures began to seem. Now, there was little popular support for what was left of the revolution, for democracy or institution-building, plurality, freeing political prisoners or, especially, the right to protest.

In late June 2014, as all Egypt was absorbed in the Brazil World Cup, blissfully forgetful of struggle and upheaval, twenty-three young activists were arrested for demonstrating against the anti-protest law. When he heard the news, Amr was overcome with frustration—but not with the regime. To him it was one more demonstration of the insularity and self-indulgence of the liberal activists, forever being outmaneuvered by tougher-minded forces from the Islamists to the army.

"Why, exactly, were you holding this protest during the World Cup?" he typed furiously on Facebook, as his friends lamented the imprisonments. "It shows how out of touch you are with ordinary people. Even the human rights lawyers who have to come and get you out of jail just want to stay at home and watch the football. If you really want people to support you and believe in you, wait until the weather gets cooler, then have a protest about electricity shortages."

Despite the promises of "Good Omen," many thought about leaving Egypt. Every week now, educated young men, friends of friends with degrees in business or law, contacted me for advice and help on reaching the West. Used to the Egyptian system of *wasta*, they were crestfallen and disbelieving when I told them there was nothing I could do—no one I could call at the British Embassy, no strings I could pull in London, to get special consideration for their visa applications. Those without the education, money and contacts for legal channels were taking more desperate measures. Men from the poor villages of the delta and Upper Egypt were traveling to work in Libya, disregarding the chaos and violence of the civil war, or trusting people smugglers on a more dangerous journey. In 2013, more than twenty-seven hundred Egyptians had been recorded arriving illegally in Europe by sea, making the perilous crossing of the Mediterranean in open boats alongside Eritreans, Somalians and Syrians fleeing the civil war.[5]

Amr, as organized as ever, was finalising his emigration to Canada. That autumn I dropped in to see him at a hospital where he was completing the medical checks required for his skilled-worker visa. Despite all his qualifications, the process had already taken four years, and his nerves were frayed by the long wait and uncertainty.

"Look at me," he said angrily. "I'm a software engineer, I speak three languages, I could make money for Egypt. But I feel like persona non grata in my own country." He counted the points off on his fingers. "I don't have any freedom, I don't have any rights, I can't even do my job efficiently. I have to leave. And the trap is closing on us."

Since the revolution and the unrest that followed, it had become increasingly difficult for even the most educated to emigrate. Amr's closest friend, a software engineer from a Christian family, had just claimed asylum in the United States—a drastic but increasingly common step for Egyptian Christians, atheists and political activists who could claim to fear repression at home. Even tourist visas to Western countries, formerly granted after a lengthy and demeaning process requiring bank statements and letters from an employer, were drying up. One of Amr's colleagues, having submitted all the documentation for an expensive holiday to New Zealand, had just been refused a visa with a humiliating email:

We noted that you are a single Egyptian male. At this time we note the current deteriorating economic, political and security/safety climate in Egypt as this is considered to significantly affect your incentives to return to your place of residence and therefore reduces your personal circumstances.

The nurse managing the medical checks slouched up to us with a file of documents for signing, her expression sullen. But when Amr handed the file back to her, her face brightened.

"Sir, we'll speed you through these checks as fast as possible, don't worry," she said and bustled off.

Amr saw me look after her, puzzled. "I tucked LE50 in the file," he said simply.

"You can't bribe a nurse!" I said, horrified.

He laughed at my expression. "You've been here this long, and you're still thinking like a European. You know this is the only way to get anything done."

I looked at him. Despite his cynical veneer I knew he loved his friends and his hometown, and could guess what a wrench it would be for him to start a new life in a distant country he had never even visited.

"Do you think you'll be happier when you leave?" I asked.

He shrugged as though the question was irrelevant. "No one wants to leave his own country. But look around you. It's not that we'll have problems in the future, we're in the middle of them and it's going to get worse. Infrastructure, electricity, economy, terrorism, repression, corruption, mob rape, population explosion, the list goes on. This ship is sinking and I have to jump." He rubbed his arm where the blood sample had been taken. "I'll tell it to you straight.

The shitty 2004 Mubarak version of Egypt is a nostalgic memory now."

After the final X-ray, I walked with Amr back to where he had left his car opposite the hospital. As he reversed, an unofficial parking guard ran over, banged on his window and demanded extra money. These self-appointed guards were part of the city's huge informal economy, working patches of curbside, collecting bribes and orchestrating a complex system of double and triple parking.

"I already paid you, when I arrived," Amr told him. "Once is enough."

The guard unleashed a torrent of foul imprecations against Amr's mother, to which Amr shouted furiously back.

Two local toughs leaning on a shiny 4x4 came over to intervene.

"What's going on? Why are you shouting at this old man?" one demanded.

"Nothing," said Amr sharply. "This guy is trying to steal from me and cursing me. And the whole thing is none of your business."

The man leaned in the open driver's window and punched Amr hard in the face. When Amr turned round, one eye was swollen shut and blood was pouring from a gash over his eyebrow.

I opened my mouth to shout at the man but Amr turned on me.

"Don't say anything. A foreigner getting involved will only make it worse."

I knew he was right. Starting an argument was as futile as going to the police. The only way to resolve the situation was to turn up later with a gang of men even tougher than those two—or to use *wasta* to have them threatened by the police or army. Doing nothing was the only realistic option. I sank back into the seat as, peering through his good eye, Amr navigated through the traffic to a hospital that was covered by his work health-care scheme. Though it was a private hospital in a middle-class area, inside it was overcrowded and dirty, the corridors choked with fainting women and sick children squatting on the floor. Wanting to help, I stretched my Arabic vocabulary on the in-house insurance clerk while Amr was stitched up by an obese, cheerful young doctor.

"I'll remember this day if I ever feel homesick in Canada," he said as he left the hospital with his head bandaged and eye blackening.

Amal and Amr, having the resources and opportunity to leave, were in a minority. Most people I knew now chose to maintain their sanity by withdrawing into their own lives. Except for the very poor and the unlucky—such as the residents of north Sinai caught between the army and the militants—it was possible to create a bubble of more-or-less normality in which you moved from safe place to safe place, surrounded by friends and family, screening out as much of the chaos as you could. It reminded me of Ayman's descriptions of his parents' attitude—"walk next to the wall"—under Mubarak, and I wondered if the generation who had risen up against Mubarak, who'd been so certain in February 2011 that they were different, really were. At first I'd been puzzled by people I knew who, after Sisi's coup, shrugged off any mention of politics, avoided talk of the future and grinned blankly if I was harassed on the street while I was with them. Now I understood they were just trying to survive.

Life was becoming a series of compromises. After years of careful planning and working to become fluent in German, Abu el-Hassan had gone to work as a junior doctor in Cologne. I was very surprised when, after only a few months, he came home.

"It wasn't what I thought it would be," he said when we went for one of our old favorite walks among the mosques. "It was hard, and so expensive, and the people were cold. Life was not good there." Now he was talking about building a traditional adobe house on some land he had bought in Luxor, under the austere tomb-dotted mountain on the west bank of the Nile, surrounding himself with beauty as insulation against all the ugliness.

Ayman, gentle and sensitive, had reluctantly taken a job in the HR department of an insurance company to help support his family. Sometimes he came round, awkward in his new suit, to drink tea with Maggie and me after work. Though he was as devout as ever, he was increasingly interested in the outside world and spent hours debating religion in international online forums. It was the opposite of his retreat into Salafism. Inspired by these conversations, in his spare time he was writing a novel about how different societies around the world treated women. He talked now about studying philosophy at Oxford, or Islamic sciences in California, and I hoped he would make it happen.

Mazen's life had also changed. As the nights drew in that autumn of 2014, I drove with him and his brother the 125 miles from Cairo to Alexandria, where they had a meeting about their family's chain of petrol stations in the Nile delta. Halfway, we stopped in the governorate of Monofeyya, the family's ancestral home, where the business was based. As we turned off the desert highway, cars were replaced by Toyota pickups. The road roughened and around us stretched crops and scrub enclosed by tumbledown fences and ditches in the dry soil.

"Fifteen or twenty years ago, you could just come out here and fence off acres of land and it would be yours," said Mazen as his brother's shiny city car lurched over the dirt. "That's what my dad did. And now this land is worth more than you can imagine."

We passed a Coptic monastery and its farmland, enclosed defensively in a miles-long blank wall so high we couldn't see in. Opposite it, a new church was being built, its slender domed towers topped with crosses.

Mazen scowled at it. "The Christians are expanding, taking over the land," he said. "They just fenced it off and took it for themselves."

"Isn't that what you just said your dad did?" I asked, smiling at his inconsistency.

"This is different," he said stubbornly. "Why should we have to hear their church bells and see their crosses?" It was the kind of complaint I'd expect to hear from hard-line Islamists, whose media portrayed Egyptian Christians as *kelab Tawadros*, the dogs of the Coptic pope Tawadros, an enemy within. But I knew that while Mazen hated Sisi as much as the Islamists did, he criticized the Brotherhood too. Copts were simply an easier target for the frustration it was hard to act out against anyone else.

We stopped off at the family villa, abandoned and derelict since their father had moved to Saudi Arabia. In the overgrown garden, oranges were dropping from the trees to rot in the dry grass. Mazen and I balanced some on a heap of rubble and took potshots at them with the air rifle he had brought with him. As he laughed at my wild shooting, for the first time the weight seemed to drop from his shoulders. These days Mazen looked years older than the idealistic graduate I'd met before the revolution. His face was set in disillusioned lines and his voice had an unhappy, cynical tone. His father had stymied his attempts to join his sister and her family in Australia, and he was trying to find a way to avoid being permanently drawn into the family business. In the meantime, he was setting up his own business with his brother, importing women's accessories from China. When we got back on the highway, they argued about whether it was Islamically acceptable for them to sell women's clothing, or whether sticking to sparkly mobile phone covers was safer.

In Alexandria, the brothers dropped off an unmarked envelope with a man from the local government who had smoothed their way through some red tape. He nodded and smiled his way through pleasantries over tea, his eyes hooded. It was the same way business had worked under Mubarak.

"It's a consideration," said Mazen's brother as we sat on the tumbled concrete blocks that lined Alexandria's seafront afterward, breathing in the fresh air off the Mediterranean before we returned to the smog of Cairo. Both brothers looked relieved now the day's business was done. "You have to recognize their help. Unfortunately, this is the only way things work here. We have to keep running, look after our employees, pay people's salaries. And these people have the power to shut you down if you don't keep them happy."

Mazen grimaced, then stood up on his block and stretched his arms wide, facing the sun where it was sinking into the western sea in a blaze of orange and violet.

"*Subhanallah*, glory to God," he said, but he sounded less uplifted than angry. "When we look from all the ugliness humans create"—he spun around to take in the cheap, ugly tower blocks and the traffic snarled along the seafront, and I was sure he was thinking of the "consideration" too—"to that beauty, we can easily see God is the only real thing in our lives."

I looked south to where Egypt stretched out under the darkening sky and thought about the impossible situation the country put its young people in. They could play along with bribery, corruption and *wasta*, or see their businesses fail, their families struggle and their health, safety and opportunities compromised. That kind of martyrdom, for all but the very few, held no rewards.

As we drove back toward Cairo, weaving around the traffic accidents, checkpoints and roadworks that blocked the highway, the delta farmland unrolling to either side in the dark, the conversation turned to Islamic State. A young man the same age as Mazen called Islam Yaken, from the same wealthy district of Cairo, had just been identified in photos of a wild-haired militant riding a horse and wielding a sword like a medieval warrior. He had once been a girl-chasing gym fanatic who posted Facebook pictures of his bare muscular torso. Now people were calling him the "hipster jihadi."

"If you go off this road to either side, I guarantee everyone will support Daesh and believe they're fighting to protect Islam," Mazen's brother said, using the Arabic acronym for Islamic State.

"But how come people are ready to believe the Brotherhood are terrorists, if the state tells them so, while they still support Daesh?" I asked.

Mazen's brother shrugged. "First, some of them do support the Brotherhood. Second, we don't know that Daesh are real. There's no proof of what's really going on there, and there's a lot of manipulation by the Western media," he said. "Hollywood tricks. These beheading videos could easily be faked in a studio." It was a slight variation on an argument I had heard many times. I was frustrated by the baroque conspiracy theories voiced by clever, educated people, and they in turn were disappointed by my weak-minded general belief in events reported by the BBC, *New York Times* or *Guardian.* When I looked at the mainstream Egyptian media, with its open bias and disregard for facts, I could almost understand why.

"What do you think is the truth, then?"

"For me it's obvious," he said. "Daesh has been created by Israel and the United States to discredit Muslims and provide the West with another excuse to invade and seize the oil."

What sounded to me like a fringe conspiracy theory was, in Egypt, a generally accepted truth. When I switched on my computer at home, my friends were sharing a cartoon of an Islamic State jihadi puppet operated by the figures of a leering, hook-nosed Jew and Uncle Sam.

The paranoia was carefully stoked by the state and pro-Sisi media. Back in Cairo, I went to a government press conference on terrorism that—in a sign of the times—was led not by a politician or academic but by a TV presenter. From the eerily lit studio of his show *Black Box*, Abdelrahim Ali claimed to uncover conspiracies against Egypt orchestrated by improbable permutations of the Brotherhood, Hamas, al-Qaeda, foreign spies and mysterious "fifth columnists." Now the revolution against Mubarak had been added to the scapegoats, and the protests against the brutality of the police and security services recast as attempts to destroy the fabric of the state. As "proof" of the revolutionaries' moral degradation, Abdelrahim Ali broadcast illegally recorded private phone calls between young activists as they discussed women.[6] How he had access to these recordings was unclear—he would say only "a good journalist protects his sources"—but he was widely suspected of being an informer for state security.

When Abdelrahim Ali stepped up to the podium, the menace in the hotel conference room where we had gathered was almost tangible.

"There are international conspiracies aimed at destroying Arab states, the biggest of which is of course Egypt," he announced to the media and academics gathered amid the white tablecloths, bottled water and velour stacking chairs. "If we look at Syria and Iraq, the same scenario is emerging in Egypt." This was the worst fear of every Egyptian. Terrorist attacks, though increasing, were still limited in scope. There was little prospect of civil war, sectarian slaughter or hordes of invading jihadis. But amid worsening regional chaos, "at least we're not Iraq or Syria" had become a means of excusing everything Sisi did.[7]

"There has been chaos following January 25, 2011," Abdelrahim Ali continued, raising his eyebrows meaningfully at the audience, who sat silent and spellbound. "The weakening of the security apparatus was intended by those who contributed to January 25, who tried to bring down the interior ministry. The so-called Arab Spring was intended to destroy states and regimes. Instead of fighting each other openly, hostile states send terrorists to destroy your state while keeping their own army and citizens safe—what we call fourth-generation warfare." This concept, much beloved of Sisi and his officials, meant that in practice anyone who opposed the state could be identified as a "terrorist." The swallowing up of the popular protests of January 25, 2011 by the military-orchestrated spectacle of June 30, 2013 seemed complete.

A middle-aged woman in a headscarf and bright turquoise nail polish shouted a question in a high angry voice. It was the same theory voiced by Mazen's brother.

"Is Islamic State supported by the United States to threaten the Arabs? I know they're supported by Qatar because the Qataris want to destroy the Egyptian state."

"There have been plans to destroy this country for years, I've talked about them on my program," replied Abdelrahim Ali, nodding. Aware, doubtless, that Egypt was still dependent on U.S. aid, he left the plotters' identity unspecified. "There is a conspiracy to destroy the country and the region, to break the spinal cord—the army—of Middle Eastern states. The conspiracy against Egypt was tackled by June 30 and the removal of Mohamed Morsi."

As if the Brotherhood and foreign conspirators were insufficient as public enemies, the regime was turning on unwanted minorities who had nothing to do with terrorism. In December, police arrested twenty-six allegedly gay men in a public bathhouse, herding them half-naked into the street while a pro-regime journalist filmed the scene on her mobile phone. Their prospects in detention were grim, as police doctors practiced forced rectal examinations that they claimed could identify "habitual homosexuals." The next month, police shut down what they described as an "atheist cafe" in downtown Cairo, in line with a joint campaign by the ministries of youth and religious endowments to eradicate atheism in Egypt. Though no one was sure how they had arrived at the figure, al-Azhar scholars had just announced that Egypt had the highest population of atheists in the Arab world—866 of its 85 million people.[8] Abu el-Hassan laughed. "I probably know that many myself," he said.

The students were being shut down too. In January I met Youssof, the student activist from al-Azhar, who was preparing for his final university exams. Between study sessions, he was ferrying textbooks and practice papers to his imprisoned friends, who had been transferred from far-off Abu Zaabal prison to Tora prison in central Cairo in order to sit their finals too. By now, there were about seven hundred students from the Cairo branch of al-Azhar University in detention, and the university was sending exam papers and teaching staff to the prison to invigilate the exams.

"How can they just send the exam papers and not do anything to support their students?" I asked.

"Oh, al-Azhar used to do this in my dad's day, for people imprisoned by Sadat," said Youssof cheerfully. "And before that under Nasser. The university has a lot of experience with this. And the state's pragmatic too—they imprison students, but they still let them do their exams."

"So you have to keep going to Tora to deliver their books?"

He laughed. "No way. I go and visit them all the time, but I only take them books right before the exams. This is the Egyptian way of studying. I'm not in jail, I can get books whenever I like, and I don't study all year round!" He sighed. "My best friend is in the same faculty as me, studying simultaneous interpretation. He'll graduate in jail."

On the eve of the fourth anniversary of the uprising against Mubarak, in the middle of downtown Cairo, police shot dead Shaimaa el-Sabbagh, an unarmed leftist activist who was holding a wreath of flowers she planned to place in Tahrir Square to honor those killed in the revolution. A fellow protester was arrested on suspicion of shooting her, and pro-Sisi media suggested the Brotherhood was responsible. On the same day, a seventeen-year-old girl was shot dead by police at an Islamist anti-Sisi rally in Alexandria. They were two additions to the lengthening list of the revolution's dead. Some had become icons: Khaled Said, beaten to death in an Alexandria stairwell. The Coptic activist Mina Daniel, shot at Maspero. The al-Azhar scholar Emad Effat, the "sheikh of the revolution," shot in Tahrir. And less famous people like Moez, the conscript soldier whose family I had met, who was shot and stabbed outside Ismailia. Four years after the revolution, citizens were still at the mercy of the state. Their lives were cheap, and few even agreed on who was worth mourning. In early 2011, the revolution's dead—who Shaimaa el-Sabbagh had been on her way to commemorate—had been hailed as sacred martyrs for freedom and justice, their sacrifice a stepping stone to a better future. Now, it was getting harder to believe that anyone's death could achieve anything at all.

In March 2015 I sat cross-legged on the scuffed parquet floor of my apartment in Cairo, sorting my possessions in preparation for moving out. I didn't have very much—a bag of clothes, a few Arabic books and my laptop. Maggie was moving to the center of town, closer to her Arabic school, so she could take the colorful glassware and the traditionally patterned cushions and throws that we'd bought in street markets and that made our landlady's eyes bulge with horror when she came to collect the rent.

"She's thinking, *What hideous orientalist kitsch*," Abu el-Hassan explained helpfully, crossing his long legs on the sofa.

"Hideous?" said Maggie in outrage. "We're not the ones who put gold rococo furniture everywhere. Or yards of brown velour curtains."

Abu el-Hassan spread his hands. "My dear, I love the traditional handicrafts of Egypt. Unfortunately most of my countrymen feel differently."

I left them bickering amicably and went to sift through the pile of notebooks in my room, the records of interviews with Egyptian politicians, religious scholars, TV stars and ordinary men and women dating back years. I'd been proud of my hard-won knowledge about Egypt. Along the way I'd got many things wrong—people still laughed about a cafe I'd taken to visiting every night during the summer of 2010, because I could always get a table and nobody bothered me when I sat alone, though the waiters eyed me a little strangely. Eventually I found out it was a notorious meeting place for prostitutes and their clients, summer visitors from the Gulf.

But eventually I felt confident of having accumulated not just facts and practical survival skills, but subtler abilities—knowing, more or less, the right polite stock phrases to use, when to joke, when to make a sideways reference to an old song or saying that would make everyone laugh with surprised recognition, how to gauge what someone might reasonably be expected to think or say or do in any given situation.

I had listened for so many hours to people talking about sex, money, religion, politics and family that I'd thought I could understand even those views I disagreed with. For a long time I'd kept the idealism I had arrived with in 2003, believing that effort and goodwill were enough to overcome any barrier between people. Flipping back through the notebooks, I realized that even most of the miscommunications had been comic. One page recorded the moment it had dawned on me that a senior Islamist I was interviewing about points of religious doctrine was hinting, charmingly, that he was looking for a second wife, "who need not necessarily be Muslim at the moment" and "who might have a research-based profession such as journalism."

Now I thought that I had also been naive. There was so much that, because of my own experiences and beliefs, I would never truly understand. I thought of how often people referred to *youm el-din*, Judgment Day—which for them immediately conjured the helpless and terrified naked crowds invoked by a thousand Friday sermons.

"I still have nightmares about it, even though I haven't believed in it for years," Abu el-Hassan said when I asked him about it.

"I couldn't have a nightmare about Judgment Day if I tried," I said. "I just don't have those images in my mental library."

He shivered. "You're lucky. I don't think I can ever get them out."

I had been wrong when I had assumed, after Morsi's election, that moderate Islamists would lead Egypt as the generation that had overthrown Mubarak grew into their thirties and forties. The Brotherhood or those like them seemed best fitted to provide the economically modern yet socially conservative society that many seemed to want. And I couldn't see how, after their suffering under Mubarak and the violence of the revolution, young Egyptians would willingly return to life under a military dictator. Carried away by the

Islamists' confidence, and seeing the patient groundwork achieved by organizations like Life Makers, I'd felt sure that they would set the tone of the new Egypt. So when the army had returned, I was amazed by how quickly the old faith in a strongman and fear of change had resurfaced. It wasn't simply the threat of external force, but a set of beliefs inculcated in Egyptians by years of dictatorship that was doing their work for them.

Now the new-old regime was stifling everyone, reminding me of Amr's descriptions of growing up in the stagnant Egypt of the 1990s while the state fought Islamic militants along the Nile. Foreigners and journalists were objects of renewed suspicion, and I was periodically called for bizarre conversations at the ministry of information, one of which ended with the intelligence officer telling me that I'd put on too much weight. I hated the feeling of being watched and I worried for the people I interviewed as well as myself.

One afternoon, on the way home from meeting students who'd been detained for protesting, I ran the usual gauntlet of leers, obscene gestures and comments on the street and hustled into a crowded women's metro carriage with relief. In what I thought was a safe space, I relaxed my vigilance enough to put on my headphones, hang on to a strap and close my eyes. Minutes later, a hand grabbed me hard between the legs at what felt like an impossible angle. It was a man with no legs, swinging through the carriage on his hands to beg from the passengers, who had singled me out as an unveiled foreigner. He laughed, and some of the women around us laughed too. Others looked away, wincing. No one said anything to the man as he swung off, and, frozen by the grotesqueness of the situation, neither did I.

At home, I found Amr drinking tea with Maggie, and told them about my journey.

"Poverty, political repression, sexual harassment, xenophobia and state neglect," said Amr, counting them off on his fingers. "Now that's a picture of Sisi's Egypt. Not what's going on in Sharm."

Maggie raised her hands helplessly, and nodded toward the television. The news channels were all broadcasting from a lavish conference Sisi was hosting in Sharm el-Sheikh to encourage foreign investment, because the economy was permanently a few months from collapse. In Cairo, the flame-scarred shell of Mubarak's party building in Tahrir, burned by protesters during the revolution, had been concealed by a huge banner declaring "Investment is the key to Egypt's well-being." Completely implausible plans were unveiled to build a new capital city in the desert east of Cairo at a cost of $45 billion. No one at the conference mentioned the fact that parliamentary elections had just been indefinitely postponed. Tony Blair, whose rhetoric had overshadowed the start of my journey in 2003, had resurfaced to brush such concerns aside.

"Look, I'm absolutely in favor of democracy," he had reassured the delegates, who included kings and emirs, presidents and prime ministers, the U.S. Secretary of State John Kerry and Christine Lagarde of the IMF. "But I also think you've got to be realistic sometimes about the path of development."[9]

Now, as Maggie, Amr and I watched, Sisi himself took the podium.

"In the name of God, the merciful, the compassionate," he began in the traditional Islamic formula, then paused theatrically. "Forgive me, I can't say anything without the young people who helped organize this event. With your permission."

As if released from a starting gate, two dozen teenage and twenty-something boys and girls bounded toward the stage. They were *awlad el-nas*, the sons and daughters of the upper class, immaculately groomed, clear-skinned, shiny-haired and beaming. The boys wore suits, the girls chic Western-style skirts and tops that would be impossible to wear on the street in central Cairo, their hair flowing. Only one wore a headscarf. It was Gamal Mubarak's vision of Egypt's youth—wealthy, privately educated, secular and compliant—come true.

Sisi disappeared in a welter of flying hair and jostling shoulders, his bodyguard pawing ineffectually at the crush. The girls were squealing as if they were at a pop concert.

"The greatest president in the world!" one of the boys shouted.

"I want a selfie with you!" begged a girl.

"OK sweetie, I'll take selfies with all of you," said Sisi, raising his palms mock-helplessly.

They arranged themselves round him, smartphones aloft. "Get into the picture everyone!"[10]

The next morning, I opened my laptop to read one of the girls declaring that meeting the president had transformed her life. In this new era, Egypt's youth had a brighter future than ever.

"After this selfie," she announced, "I got four marriage proposals and three job offers."[11]

Epilogue

In April 2015 I finally left Egypt. Watching the sun rise sharp and golden over the desert as I waited to board the plane, I thought of the people who had recently looked out of the same airport windows.

In the past year, two dozen of the young professionals I knew had left the country. Software developers, civil engineers and doctors, arts administrators, human rights workers and political researchers, they were all in their mid-twenties to mid-thirties. They had scattered across the world, from Saudi Arabia, Qatar and Lebanon, to Sweden, Germany and Switzerland, and Australia, Canada and the United States—compromising on salaries, residency status and location because of their certainty that Egypt held no future for them. Of the people I had written about, Amr was waiting for the confirmation of his Canadian visa, and Amal was planning to return to China with her Irish husband and new baby. Egypt was facing a brain drain, and through corruption and repression it was the regime that was pushing away the people it most needed to rebuild the country. Even Wael Ghonim, the young Google executive who had created the We Are All Khaled Said Facebook page, had said he could not return as "Egypt no longer welcomes those who are like me."[1]

I was leaving too, because foreigners and journalists were also under pressure, and working was becoming increasingly difficult for me and dangerous for those I interviewed. I had traveled between the UK and Egypt many times since that first journey in 2003, but this time there was an unsettling feeling of permanence to the move. For days, staying in a London apartment borrowed from a friend who was working abroad, I was disoriented without the sounds of car horns, *mahraganat* music, fireworks, feral cat fights, the shouts of street vendors and microbus conductors and the call to prayer punctuating my days and nights. I couldn't get used to wearing T-shirts or short skirts, or to relaxing my constant vigilance for harassers, secret police or spying neighbors. My dreams were a confused jumble of Arabic and English. I couldn't make sense of the move from pressure, threat and chaos to order, calm and plenty.

Twelve years on, it seemed that when it came to the Middle East the UK had learned little since 2003. Exporting "the universal values of the human spirit," as Blair had prescribed then, had failed bloodily and spectacularly. The state-building zeal of the Western spies and diplomats I'd met in Cairo's language schools had evaporated, and British troops had finally left Iraq and Afghanistan.

The threats they had purportedly been sent to eradicate had only multiplied in size and complexity. MPs were arguing about how to stop young British men and women from traveling to join Islamic State in Syria, how to counter the spread of extremist ideology and prevent attacks by radicalized Britons at home, and how to deal with the thousands of refugees—not only from Syria but also from Iraq, Afghanistan, Somalia, Eritrea and elsewhere—arriving each week in Europe. The solutions they proposed were also little different from those of 2003. Britain might be more wary of committing ground troops, but it had bombed Libya, was bombing Iraq and MPs looked likely to vote for airstrikes in Syria too. The former British foreign secretary William Hague remarked, as if oblivious of the results of all contemporary and colonial intervention in the Middle East, that "if communities and leaders cannot live peacefully together in Syria and Iraq then we will have to try them living peacefully but separately in the partition of those countries."[2]

The promise of the Arab Spring as it had appeared for those brief exhilarating months in 2011 had collapsed. The power of the old dictators had been broken—Gaddafi was dead; Ben Ali in exile in Saudi Arabia; Assad clinging on in Damascus having lost control of two-thirds of his country; Saleh on the wrong side of a civil war in Yemen; and Mubarak in limbo in a military hospital in Cairo, with his democratically elected successor Morsi in prison nearby. But there was war in Libya, Yemen, Iraq and Syria. Tunisia, though politically more stable, had become the largest source of foreign fighters joining Islamic State, and sixty people had been shot dead in two jihadi attacks on Western tourists in April and June.

It was easy, seeing the intractable suffering in the region and confronted by the return of authoritarianism under Sisi in Egypt, to be overtaken by despair. But when I looked at the young people I'd written about, I saw cause for hope.

The revolution of 2011 and its aftermath had shaped them all. Sara and Ruqayah had experienced violence and trauma at the hands of the state; Mazen and Youssof had repeatedly risked their lives to resist it. Everyone had witnessed the power and solidarity of truly popular protest, and the first free elections in Egypt's history. They had heard liberals, religious ultraconservatives and all parties in between debate their views on politics and society in public. They had seen their former dictator Mubarak standing trial and sentenced to imprisonment. They had tasted, however briefly, freedom, possibility and self-respect.

These experiences hadn't yet resulted in the freedom everyone had at first expected and hoped for, that Mazen's joyful shout of "We did it!" had welcomed. But in a way I still thought he was right—things in Egypt would never be the same again. An awareness that things could be different had been planted and at some point it would bear fruit.

The conditions that had underpinned the 2011 revolution— spreading access to the free space of the Internet, resentment at police brutality, frustration with unemployment, poverty, stasis and the lack of political opportunity—were still in place. And the state faced future demands there was no sign it could fulfill. By 2030, Egypt's population would reach 116 million, a more than 40% increase on 2012.[3] Pressure on water, food, energy, infrastructure and public services—all already inadequate—was growing.

Sisi had been riding high at the conference in March 2015 when he had gathered the young people for the staged selfie session. Powerful delegates from the Gulf States, Europe and the United States had gathered to endorse his vision of Egypt as an investment hub. But as the year wore on, his position looked increasingly precarious. He could no longer rely on blank financial and political checks from Saudi Arabia and the Emirates, and the default support of the West.

With a new leader—King Salman had succeeded his brother King Abdullah in January, though his son Mohammed bin Salman was suspected to wield much of the power—Saudi Arabia's foreign policies were shifting. Despite lavish financial and political assistance, Egypt had failed to demonstrate its gratitude by joining bombing campaigns in Yemen, where Saudi Arabia was targeting Iranian-backed Shia Houthi militias. As the kingdom cooled toward Egypt, it was warming toward Egypt's rival, Turkey, whose assistance Saudi Arabia needed in the intractable proxy war against Bashar al-Assad, also backed by Iran, in Syria.

Sisi had removed Morsi and had himself elected president by pledging to maintain security. But Sinai Province, the group of militants who had pledged allegiance to Islamic State, were operating in Sinai and on the Egyptian mainland, and had kidnapped and killed at least two foreigners along with scores of police and soldiers. The state looked increasingly incompetent to handle the threat. In September, one of the Egyptian military's Apache helicopter gunships, hunting militants in the Western Desert, gunned down twelve people including eight Mexican tourists picnicking at a popular scenic area. Officials falsely claimed that the party had entered a restricted area without a permit, while the media obediently commented that the victims, being Mexicans, were surely smugglers and gun-runners.

In November, a Russian passenger plane with 224 people on board fell out of the sky shortly after taking off from Sharm el-Sheikh. The Egyptian authorities mishandled this disaster too, delaying making an official statement for weeks, while the media reported speculation that the plane had been bombed as a conspiracy against Egyptian tourism and Sinai Province claimed responsibility for the act. Only after the UK halted flights to and from Sharm el-Sheikh and Russia confirmed that the plane had been destroyed by a device smuggled onboard at the airport, where security was notoriously lax, did Egypt respond. The huge sums of money injected into the regime by Gulf States had failed to produce results, and Egypt's international partners' patience was running out. If a security state couldn't deliver security, there was little reason for it to exist.

At home, Sisi's popularity was also waning. Turnout in the parliamentary elections of November 2015 was embarrassingly low, even after the president appeared on TV to personally beg voters to demonstrate their support. His rule seemed increasingly unlikely to match Mubarak's thirty-year balancing act; the old tools of repression were increasingly inadequate to contain a huge population that had known days of greater freedom.

In November, Amr gathered with his friends in an old bar in Alexandria. He was about to emigrate to Canada, and he wanted one last night out in his hometown. The Spitfire was a remnant of the city's Second World War watering holes, with smoke-darkened walls, a jumble of vintage posters and five or six rickety tables usually crammed with the hard-drinking regulars Amr knew well—leftist intellectuals, wealthy Christians and plumbers celebrating the start of the weekend with a cocktail of cheap brandy and Viagra. But he hadn't been to the bar for five or six months, and tonight he found it full of unfamiliar young faces.

"Who are all these kids?" he asked.

"They're students," said his friend Mahmoud. "The place is full of them these days."

Amr looked around. Ordinary middle-class teenage boys and girls were sitting together, laughing and flirting, relaxed about sitting in the "unrespectable" space of a bar. They weren't arguing about art or politics like the regulars, they were just enjoying a night out. "What's that they're drinking?"

"Stella Lemon—it's lemon-flavored beer, one of those alcopop things."

"OK, now I'm really feeling old. In our day it was a bottle of local gin on the seafront, then vomiting your guts out and lying on the rocks till you sobered up. It wasn't a lifestyle accessory, for God's sake!"

"This is it, man," said Mahmoud, slapping him on the back. "We're no longer the younger generation. This is the new generation. It's their country now."

Amr had just turned thirty-six. He looked at the nineteen and twenty-year-olds drinking around him, looking for a night of fun and forgetfulness from the stress of living in Egypt. They wanted to enjoy their lives and they were defying their fear of their parents, of state security, of religious and social censure. And that, he thought, might make them harder to control.

The barman, who had known Amr and his friends since they were teenagers, leaned across the bar. "Here's your old favorite, Amr. Have a good journey," he said, and cued a song on the stereo.

"Hey, isn't this . . ."

It was the Scorpions' "Wind of Change," the anthem of the end of the Cold War. A quarter of a century earlier Amr had heard it on the bootleg tapes sold from Alexandria's street kiosks and, only half-understanding the words, loved its promise of freedom. Then as a young man in the cafes of downtown Cairo he had listened to it again, dreaming excitedly of the communist regimes of eastern Europe toppling. Would that wave ever reach the Middle East and Egypt?

Now Amr laughed, breaking the moment of nostalgia. "Well, we did what we could. Now it's these kids' turn."

List of Main Characters

AMR (age in 2011: thirty-one) A software engineer from Alexandria, the first university-educated member of his family. Multilingual and highly skilled.

AMAL (twenty-nine) BORN to a modest family in a rural village, Amal is expected to marry young and obey her husband. Instead, she defies all convention to follow her own path.

NAYERA (twenty-six) THE daughter of middle-class parents who allow her a certain amount of freedom. Struggles to reconcile double standards for men and women in sex and relationships.

ABDEL RAHMAN (twenty-seven) From a tribal village in southern Egypt, moves in fashionable media circles in Cairo but has kept his traditional views about women and marriage.

MAZEN (twenty-three) A fan of the TV preacher Amr Khaled and a dedicated volunteer in his youth development movement. Unexpectedly finds himself in the front line of the protests during the revolution.

AYMAN (twenty-three) As a devout teenager, serious, thoughtful Ayman chooses to follow ultraconservative Salafi Islam—to the horror of his respectable upper-middle-class parents.

ABU EL-HASSAN (twenty-seven) Growing up in a traditional religious family in a village outside Cairo, Abu el-Hassan memorizes the Quran by the age of twelve. After graduating as a doctor, he becomes an atheist—but is unable to share his beliefs with his family, friends or colleagues.

RUQAYAH (thirteen) A student at an Islamic high school in Cairo, Ruqayah acts as a security guard for the Rabaa protest camp in 2013, facing death or detention for her convictions.

SARA (nineteen) A student at al-Azhar University in Cairo, Sara loses her fiancé during the Rabaa massacre in 2013—which cements her determination to take action against the regime.

Some Public Figures

HOSNI MUBARAK   Former air force officer and president of Egypt from 1981 to 2011. Married to the half-Welsh Suzanne Mubarak and father of the former banker Gamal Mubarak, who the family hopes will succeed his father.

MOHAMED MORSI   SENIOR Muslim Brother who becomes president of Egypt in June 2012. A previously little-known figure elected after more popular Brotherhood candidates are disqualified.

ABDEL FATTAH   el-sisi   One-time head of military intelligence and member of the Military Council that takes power after Mubarak's overthrow. Appointed defense minister by Mohamed Morsi in August 2012, seizes power from him in July 2013 and is elected president in June 2014.

KHALED SAID   TWENTY-EIGHT-YEAR-OLD man from Alexandria beaten to death in a stairwell by police in June 2010.

WAEL GHONIM   YOUNG Egyptian Google executive based in Abu Dhabi who sets up a Facebook page called We Are All Khaled Said, calling for protest against police brutality.

AMR KHALED   MODERATE TV preacher who rises to fame in the early 2000s and is forced to leave Egypt by the security services. Stars in the influential religious TV series *Life*

Makers, which inspires youth organizations across the Arab world.

MOHAMED HASSAN   CONSERVATIVE Salafi preacher who founds his own TV channel and becomes a media sensation across the Middle East.

A Note on Names

Egyptians are people of many names. Everyone's state ID card carries at least four, and usually five. Mohamed Ahmed Ibrahim Mohamed Hassan, and his sister Doha Ahmed Ibrahim Mohamed Hassan, would be respectively Mohamed son of, and Doha daughter of, Ahmed son of Ibrahim son of Mohamed son of Hassan. Because names such as Mohamed and Ahmed are so ubiquitous, some people choose a more unusual ancestral name—such as Gaafar—either to use as their surname or to replace their own first name. Others may also have a family name, such as el-Naggar, which they may or may not choose to use.

To add to the confusion, many people are also known to family, friends and even colleagues by common nicknames or contractions such as Abdou or Mido, or by a *konya*—such as Abu Hassan or Umm Hassan, father or mother of Hassan— which may refer to any children they have or, teasingly, any notable characteristics. Egyptians are also great users of honorifics, which may be related to profession—*doktor* or *bashmohandes*, engineer—or social status—*usteza*, for instance, literally means a female professor but has come to mean any educated woman. An individual may go by four or five different names in the course of a day depending on where they are and who they are with.

In this setting the Western convention of referring to an individual by their surname after the first mention makes little sense, so characters known by two names—for instance Amr Khaled or Mohamed Ibrahim—keep both throughout.

Because of the sensitive nature of their stories, the main characters are identified by their first names alone—some of which have been changed.

A Note on Arabic

As across the rest of the Arabic-speaking world, no Egyptians speak formal Arabic, the closest modern relative of the language of the Quran, as their mother tongue. Instead, they speak Egyptian, a dialect—or family of dialects—with its own grammar and vocabulary that differs from other Arabic dialects on a spectrum from Palestinian, which overlaps considerably, to Moroccan, which an Egyptian may struggle to understand.

In everyday situations formal Arabic is as out of place as trying to hail a cab in Middle English. But it is still the language of literacy: of bureaucracy, books and newspapers, some broadcasting and most religious teaching, the repository of everything official, respectable and righteous.

Though most Egyptians hate struggling with formal Arabic's labyrinthine grammar and abstruse vocabulary at school, it is hard to find anyone who would consider abandoning it altogether. It is their link to the rest of the Arab world, to Arabic's long written heritage and, most importantly of all, to the Quran. Writing in dialect is still considered ugly and vulgar, even as its use on social media has grown and a new system, Franco-Arab, has sprung up to render it in Roman letters. And though they speak it in the office, on the street and at home, Egyptians do not recognize their dialect as a language in its own right.

The Arabic that appears in this book is almost all Egyptian dialect, and is transliterated to strike a balance between being comprehensible to non-Arabic readers, and recognizable to Arabic speakers.

Timeline of Some Major Events in Egypt

1952   Nationalist army officers lead a coup against
            Egypt's British-backed monarchy with the sup-
            port of groups including the Muslim Brother-
            hood, and declare Egypt a republic.

1956   Gamal Abdel Nasser becomes president and
            Egypt is declared a single-party state. Over the
            next fourteen years he creates a pan-Arabist social-
            ist state, nationalizes the Suez Canal and pur-
            sues large-scale industrialization projects. Egypt
            becomes the political and cultural center of the
            Middle East. Nasser brutally represses political
            opponents including the Muslim Brotherhood.

1967   Nasser launches the Six Day War against Israel
            and suffers a disastrous defeat. The Sinai penin-
            sula is occupied by Israel.

1970   The former army officer Anwar Sadat becomes
            president following the death of Nasser. He reori-
            ents Egypt away from Russia and toward the West
            and begins a policy of *infitah*—economic liberali-
            zation. At the same time, he cultivates Islamists
            as a counterweight to socialist opponents.

1973   The Ramadan War with Israel ends with a
            UN-brokered cease-fire, but is hailed as a vic-
            tory by Egypt after a surprise attack into the
            Israeli-occupied Sinai.

1979	Sadat signs a peace treaty with Israel following the Camp David Accords of 1978. Israel begins to withdraw from the Sinai.
1981	Sadat is assassinated by jihadis at a military parade in Cairo. His vice president Hosni Mubarak, who was wounded in the attack, becomes president. He cracks down on Islamists, but during the 1990s a radical insurgency grows in the Nile Valley, culminating in the 1997 massacre of tourists at a temple in Luxor.
2002–3	Protests begin in major Egyptian cities against first the Israeli assault on the West Bank during the second Palestinian intifada, then the coalition invasion of Iraq. Some express discontent with Mubarak himself.
2005	The opposition movement Kefaya organizes protests against the heir apparent Gamal Mubarak. Mubarak is pressured to hold the first multi-candidate presidential elections. His opponent Ayman Nour wins 8% of the vote and is imprisoned.
2010	
JUNE	Twenty-eight-year-old Khaled Said is beaten to death by police officers in Alexandria.
DECEMBER	Mohamed Bouazizi, a vegetable seller, sets himself on fire in Sidi Bouzid, Tunisia. Protests against the Tunisian regime of Zine al-Abidine Ben Ali begin.

2011

JANUARY 15   Ben Ali is forced from power and flees Tunisia for Saudi Arabia. Opposition social media pages in Egypt call for protests against police brutality on January 25, National Police Day.

JANUARY 25   Anti-regime protests take place in cities including Cairo, Alexandria, Aswan, Ismailia and Suez. Thousands of protesters converge on Tahrir Square in central Cairo.

JANUARY 28   Tens of thousands join protests across Egypt, and at least twenty-five are killed and hundreds injured by security forces. The government shuts down Internet and mobile networks across the country. Senior members of the Muslim Brotherhood are detained. The Cairo headquarters of the ruling National Democratic Party are burned, and Mubarak appears on state television, calling protests "part of a bigger plot to shake the stability" of Egypt. Police withdraw from the streets, the army is deployed to secure Cairo and a curfew is imposed.

JANUARY 29   Mubarak appoints Omar Suleiman, head of Egyptian intelligence, vice president. Following the withdrawal of the police, local residents create "people's committees" to protect their neighborhoods.

FEBRUARY 1   The largest marches of the uprising take place across Egypt. Mubarak makes an emotional speech proclaiming that he had never planned to stand in the next presidential elections in September 2011, and vowing to die on Egyptian soil.

FEBRUARY 2 Gangs of thugs hired by the state, riding horses and camels, attack protesters in Tahrir in "the Battle of the Camel." Eleven protesters are killed and more than six hundred injured. Internet and mobile networks are restored.

FEBRUARY 3–10 Protests continue. Workers' strikes and sit-ins hit industrial towns. Wael Ghonim, a Google employee and administrator of the We Are All Khaled Said Facebook page, is released after eleven days in state security custody and interviewed on live TV.

FEBRUARY 11 Omar Suleiman announces that Mubarak has stepped down and power has been transferred to the Supreme Council of the Armed Forces, SCAF, led by seventy-five-year-old Field Marshal Mohamed Hussein Tantawi.

OCTOBER Twenty-eight people are killed when security forces attack a protest march calling for equal rights for Egypt's Christian minority at Maspero in Cairo.

NOVEMBER Protesters calling for an end to military rule clash with security forces in Mohamed Mahmoud Street off Tahrir Square. Fifty are killed over a week of fighting. The first free parliamentary elections begin.

2012

JANUARY   The new Muslim Brotherhood-dominated parliament is sworn in. Salafis are the second-largest group of MPs; liberal and revolutionary parties are negligible. Out of 498 elected MPs, only eight are women.

JUNE 14   Parliament is dissolved by the old regime-controlled supreme court, which rules its election unconstitutional.

JUNE 30   The Muslim Brotherhood's candidate Mohamed Morsi is sworn in as Egypt's first civilian president, after a final-round election runoff with the Mubarak-era prime minister Ahmed Shafiq.

AUGUST   Morsi removes Tantawi, the former interim military leader, as defense minister and replaces him with Abdel Fattah el-Sisi, a relatively young general known for his piety.

NOVEMBER   Morsi issues a presidential decree giving himself sweeping new powers. Pro- and anti-Brotherhood protesters clash in major cities.

2013

MAY   The Tamarod ("Rebel") opposition movement collects signatures calling for early presidential elections and calls for anti-Morsi protests in June.

JUNE 30   Hundreds of thousands to millions of Egyptians take to the streets against Morsi in army-sanctioned demonstrations. There are smaller pro-Morsi protests. Following the protests the army announces a forty-eight-hour deadline for Morsi to resolve the political crisis. Morsi's supporters set up protest camps at Rabaa Square and al-Nahda Square in Cairo.

JULY 3   The defense minister Abdel Fattah el-Sisi announces that Morsi has been removed from the presidency and the constitution has been suspended.

AUGUST 14   Security forces storm pro-Morsi protest camps at Rabaa and al-Nahda, killing around one thousand protesters. In the wave of repression that follows, the Muslim Brotherhood is declared a terrorist organization and street protest is banned. Coptic churches are burned and police and army installations targeted in retaliation for the clearances. A Sinai-based jihadi group calling itself Supporters of Jerusalem begins attacks on regime targets.

2014

JUNE   Sisi is elected president with 93% of the vote. His only opponent, the leftist Hamdeen Sabahi, gets 3%.

NOVEMBER   Supporters of Jerusalem pledges allegiance to Islamic State and renames itself Sinai Province. It kills scores of security personnel in a series of attacks.

2015

FEBRUARY   Twenty-one Egyptian Coptic migrant workers kidnapped in Libya are beheaded by Islamic State. Egypt launches airstrikes on Libya in retaliation.

MARCH   Sisi hosts an international investment conference in Sharm el-Sheikh, welcoming high-level delegates from the Gulf and the West. He receives multibillion-dollar pledges of support and announces the construction of a new capital city.

SEPTEMBER   Eight Mexican tourists are among twelve people mistakenly killed in an Egyptian army anti-terror operation in the Western Desert.

NOVEMBER   A Russian plane with 224 people on board is blown out of the sky soon after leaving Sharm el-Sheikh airport. Sinai Province claims responsibility for the bombing.

Acknowledgments

Writing this book was a far larger undertaking than I expected and I would never have completed it without the help and support of many people. Special thanks to:

The Winston Churchill Memorial Trust, Jamie Balfour and Nick Danziger for getting me started on the journey.

Dan Trilling, Mary Fitzgerald, Andy Dickson, Sholto Byrnes and Steve Bloomfield for commissions, conversations and helping me navigate the recurring bureaucratic nightmare of Egyptian press accreditation.

Sadakat Kadri and Paul Lewis for much advice and encouragement in the early stages and for not warning me not to do it.

Sarah Savitt for wise advice and Isabel Dexter for insight and fun.

My colleagues at the *Guardian*, especially Charlotte Baxter, Mel Carvalho, Robert White, Rowan Righelato and Sarah Bolesworth—and Alice O'Keeffe for letting me write about Egypt.

My agent Catherine Clarke for her advocacy and support. Michal Shavit at Harvill Secker for believing in this project in the first place and all her insight and enthusiasm since.

My dear friends Hazel, Pete and Andrew, who have not only entertained and encouraged me over the long haul but housed and fed me too.

My parents, my grandparents and Alex, Amelia and William for fun, love and practical support, and to Andy and Zoe who hosted me so generously, so many times.

In Cape Town: Steve, Morgan, Gabriel, Kili and Meru for giant encouragement, hospitality, love and adventures from the very beginning.

In Cairo, Elspeth Black was a constant source of jokes, home-made food, brave company, Arabic practice and soda water. We shared a lot of the experiences that went into this book. Thanks, Elspeth.

This book would not exist without the generosity of countless people in Egypt who shared their stories, time, knowledge and company with me over the years. Special thanks to Ahmed Hayman, Ahmed Reda, Zakaria Ibrahim, Michael Whitewood, Amr Medhat, Anas Sultan, Deana Shabaan, Nayrouz Abouzid, Osama Yusuf, Penelope Fidas, Remon Amin, Mohamed Gamal, Hassan el-Naggar, Havra Marketwala, Laura Dean, Jay Visbal, Valentina Primo, Belal Darder, Jeff Allen, Sherif el-Ghazouly, Farah Soames, Nagia Said, Mohamed Tolba, Enas el-Masry, Etaa el-Hosseiny, Maryam Metwally, Keith Lane, Ezzat Amin, Hazem Yassin, Wael Elshahat, Youssef Rakha, Samir Saad, Mette Nielsen, Mona Adel and Adel Emara, Mahmoud Abd Elmageed, Zap Tharwat, Hany al-Shafie, Mohamed Yehia and especially to E, A, H and my younger brother Youssof.

Finally, *teslam eidak* to MG for unswerving kindness and friendship. And *merci awy* to MA for limitless patience and solidarity, and for all the laughs.

Notes

PROLOGUE

1   Simon Jeffery, "Key Quotes: Tony Blair's Speech to U.S. Congress," *Guardian*, July 18, 2003.

2   Charles Levinson, "$50 Billion Later, Taking Stock of U.S. Aid to Egypt," *Christian Science Monitor*, April 12, 2004.

3   See Duncan Green, "What Caused the Revolution in Egypt?," *Guardian*, February 17, 2011.

CHAPTER 1

1   See Linda Herrera, "Downveiling: Gender and the Contest over Culture in Cairo," in Jeannie Sowers and Chris Toensing, eds., *The Journey to Tahrir: Revolution, Protest and Social Change in Egypt* (Verso, 2012), 266.

2   The exact number of Egyptian Christians is a highly politicized subject of debate. See Abdel Rahman Youssef, "Egypt's Copts: It's All in the Number," *al-Akhbar*, September 30, 2012.

3   For a detailed discussion of FGM in Egypt, see Shereen El Feki, *Sex and the Citadel: Intimate Life in a Changing Arab World* (Vintage, 2014), which helped me understand the context of the stories in this chapter.

4   World Health Organization, "Female Genital Mutilation and Other Harmful Practices," who.int.

5   Claudia Ruta, "Gender Politics in Transition: Women's Political Rights after the January 25 Revolution" (Dissertation .com, 2012), 106.

6   Michael Slackman, "In Egypt, a New Battle Begins Over the Veil," *New York Times*, January 28, 2007.

7   See Owen L. Sirrs, *A History of the Egyptian Intelligence Service* (Routledge, 2010).

8   Issandr El Amrani, "Why Tunis, Why Cairo?," *London Review of Books*, February 17, 2011.

9   Tom Chivers, "Egyptian Politicians Call for Gigimo Artificial Virginity Hymen Kit to be Banned," *Daily Telegraph*, October 6, 2009.

10   El Feki, *Sex and the Citadel*, 116.

11   Ghada Abdel Aal's popular blog, Ayza Atgawez [I Want to Get Married], which ran from 2007, explored the pressure to marry from a young woman's perspective.

12   United Nations Development Program, "Creating Opportunities," *Arab Human Development Report*, 2002.

13   World Bank, "School Enrollment, Tertiary, Gender Parity Index," worldbank.org.

CHAPTER 2

1   Maria Golia, *Cairo, City of Sand* (Reaktion, 2004), 189.

2   See Asef Bayat, "The 'Arab Street'" in Sowers and Toensing, eds., 81.

3   See Yoram Meital, "The October War and Egypt's Multiple Crossings" in Asaf Siniver, ed., *The October 1973 War: Politics, Diplomacy, Legacy* (Hurst, 2013), 66.

4   See Hossam el-Hamalawy, "Egypt's Revolution Has Been 10 Years in the Making," *Guardian*, March 2, 2011.

5   "Population and Development: The Demographic Profile of the Arab Countries," United Nations Economic and Social Commission for Western Asia, 2003.

6   See Mariz Tadros, *The Muslim Brotherhood in Contemporary Egypt: Democracy Redefined or Confined?* (Routledge, 2012), 47–49.

7   John L. Esposito, *Islam and Politics* (Syracuse University Press, 1998), 139.

8   For a detailed discussion of Nasser's wartime propaganda, see Laura James, *Nasser at War: Arab Images of the Enemy* (Palgrave Macmillan, 2006).

9   Steven A. Cook, *The Struggle for Egypt: From Nasser to Tahrir Square* (Oxford University Press, 2011), 135–37.

10 John Daniszewski, "Tales of Teen Satanism Have Egypt Inflamed," *Los Angeles Times*, February 10, 1997.

11 Jonathan Schanzer, "Gamal Mubarak: Successor Story in Egypt?," Washington Institute Policywatch, October 17, 2002.

12 "The Future of the Internet Economy in Egypt: A Statistical Profile," Arab Republic of Egypt Ministry of Communications and Information Technology, 2013.

13 "Home Computers and Internet Use in the United States," U.S. Census Bureau, September 2001.

14 Tarek Osman, *Egypt on the Brink: From Nasser to the Muslim Brotherhood* (Yale University Press, 2010), 106.

15 David Schenker, "Inside the Complex World of U.S. Military Assistance to Egypt," Washington Institute Policywatch, September 4, 2013.

16 Paul Schemm, "Egypt Struggles to Contain Anti-War Protests," *Middle East Research and Information Project*, March 31, 2003.

17 Klaus Enders, "Egypt: Reforms Trigger Economic Growth," *IMF Survey Magazine*, February 13, 2008.

18 Andrew England, "Wealth Disparities Cloud Progress," *Financial Times*, December 10, 2007.

19 Heba Handoussa et al., *Egypt Human Development Report 2010*, United Nations Development Program, 151.

20 "Poverty Driving Young to Risk Deadly Boat Journeys," IRIN News, January 16, 2008.

21 "Egypt's Torture Epidemic," Human Rights Watch, February 2004, 1.

22 Interview with Stephen Grey, *PBS Frontline World*, October 1, 2007.

23 "Ayman Nour: Profile," BBC News, December 24, 2005.

24 Issandr El Amrani, "The Murder of Khaled Said," *The Arabist*, June 14, 2010: http://arabist.net/blog/2010/6/14/the-murder-of-khaled-said.html.

CHAPTER 3

1 Khalil Alanani, "Egypt: Parliamentary Elections in the Shadow of 2000," Carnegie Endowment for International Peace, 2005.

2 Samantha M. Shapiro, "Ministering to the Upwardly Mobile Muslim," *New York Times*, April 30, 2006.

3 "Boy becomes Palestinian martyr," BBC News, October 2, 2000.

4 See "Love for a Better Life," http://love4betterlife.nicetopic.net/t49-amr-khaled-s-lecture-about-hijab.

5 The film of Nasser's 1966 speech gives a flavor of his charisma and ruthlessness: https://www.youtube.com/watch?v=Dtiat84grxw.

6 Al-Bukhari 7/541, no. 835; Muslim 3/160, no. 5268.

7 See Samuel L. Harris, "Development through Faith: The Ma'adi Life Makers and the Entrepreneurial Subject," MA thesis, Georgetown University, 2008.

8 For more on Amr Khaled and his peers' synthesis of faith and consumerism, see Patrick Haenni, *L'Islam de Marché: L'autre révolution conservatrice* (Seuil, 2005).

9   Negar Azimi, "Islam's Answer to MTV," *New York Times*, August 12, 2010.

10   *"Pop Goes Islam,"* Al Jazeera English documentary, 2011.

CHAPTER 4

1   "Egypt Bomb Kills 21 at Alexandria's Largest Church," BBC News, January 1, 2011.

2   See https://www.youtube.com/watch?v=kWr6MypZ-JU.

3   "Egypt Protests Draw Mixed Reaction in Region," CNN, January 29, 2011.

4   See https://www.youtube.com/watch?v=HjU7yAYig3U.

CHAPTER 5

1   Evan Hill and Muhammad Mansour, "Egypt's Army Took Part in Torture and Killings during Revolution, Report Shows," *Guardian*, April 10, 2013.

2   "Egypt: Military Pledges to Stop Forced 'Virginity Tests,'" *Amnesty International*, June 27, 2011.

3   "Egypt: Retry or Free 12,000 After Unfair Military Trials," Human Rights Watch, September 10, 2011.

4   Jon Leyne, "Islamists Battle for Votes in Rural Egypt," BBC News, December 14, 2011.

5   Noha el-Hennawy, "New Salafi MPs Alter Oath in Possible Sign of What's to Come," *Egypt Independent*, January 23, 2012.

6   Hania Sholkamy examined some of the causes of the fall in women's representation in parliament, after the military council abolished a quota set under Mubarak, in "Why Women Are at the Heart of Egypt's Political Trials and Tribulations," openDemocracy, January 24, 2012.

7   See https://www.youtube.com/watch?v=EgDotWRVMhk.

8   Following their "defeat" on January 28, 2011, police had largely withdrawn to their stations and the crime rate soared. See Sherif Tarek, "Egypt's Police After the Revolution: Brutality Combines with Lack of Security," Ahram Online, October 27, 2011.

9   Robert F. Worth, "Effort to Rebrand Arab Spring Backfires in Iran," *New York Times*, February 2, 2012.

10 "Egypt Salafist ex-MP Convicted of Public Indecency," BBC News, July 21, 2012.

11 See Sarah El Masry, "A Polarised Media: Religious Satellite TV Channels," *Daily News Egypt*, April 3, 2013.

12 "Egypt Court Jails Blogger Alber Saber for Blasphemy," BBC News, December 12, 2012.

13 Ahmed Ateyya, "'Rebel' Egypt Movement Defies Morsi Through Petitions," *Al-Monitor*, May 17, 2013.

14 Patrick Kingsley, "Egypt's Mohamed Morsi: I Have Made Mistakes," *Guardian*, June 26, 2013.

15 Mike Giglio, "A Cairo Conspiracy," *Daily Beast*, July 12, 2013.

CHAPTER 6

1   For a thorough and harrowing investigation of the events at Rabaa and al-Nahda squares on August 14, 2013, see the Human Rights Watch report "All According to Plan," August 12, 2014.

2   Ingy Hassieb and Jeffrey Fleishman, "Egypt Military Says Protesters Use Children as Human Shields," *Los Angeles Times*, August 2, 2013.

3   Patrick Kingsley, "Killing in Cairo: The Full Story of the Republican Guards' Club Shootings," *Guardian*, July 18, 2013.

4   Nouran el-Behairy, "El-Sisi Calls for Green Light to Fight 'Terrorism,'" *Daily News Egypt*, July 24, 2013.

5   See "All According to Plan," 81.

6   Ibid., 82.

7   Khaled Dawoud, "One Year On," *Ahram Weekly*, August 13, 2014.

8   "Egypt: Mass Attacks on Churches," Human Rights Watch, August 21, 2013.

9   Maria Abi-Habib, "Vicious Backlash Shakes One Egyptian Town," *Wall Street Journal*, August 16, 2013.

10   Andrew Marszal, "Egypt Violence: Islamists 'Execute 25 Policemen' in Sinai," *Daily Telegraph*, August 19, 2013.

11   Apart from its lack of transparency, the MB has many levels of affiliation before full membership. See Patrick Kingsley, "Muslim Brotherhood Banned by Egyptian Court," *Guardian*, September 23, 2013.

12   Mostafa Kamel, "Teslam el-Ayadi," see: https://www .youtube.com/watch?v=jDgyzOTmeiY.

13   "Six Killed in Egypt's Ismailia Attack on Military Truck," Ahram Online, October 7, 2013.

14   Safa Joudeh, "Egypt Cracks Down on Students," Al-Monitor, January 29, 2014.

15   Karim Lahidji, "Exposing State Hypocrisy: Sexual Violence by Security Forces in Egypt," report by the International Federation for Human Rights, May 2015, 7.

16   Associated Press, "Egypt's Military Leaders Unveil Devices They Claim Can Detect and Cure AIDS," *Guardian*, February 28, 2014.

17   Hussein al-Jasmi, "Boshrat Kheir," see: https://www .youtube.com/watch?v=QUBvVTNRp4Q/.

CHAPTER 7

1   Rachel Aspden, "Divide and Rule: Egypt under General Sisi," *New Humanist*, May 28, 2014.

2 Joe Stork, "Egypt's Political Prisoners," openDemocracy, March 6, 2015.

3 Patrick Kingsley, "80 Sexual Assaults in One Day—The Other Story of Tahrir Square," *Guardian*, July 5, 2013.

4 Ahmed Waguih, "Population Growth in Egypt: More People, More Problems?," Tahrir Institute for Middle East Policy, April 23, 2014.

5 Phillip Connor, "Illegal Immigration by Boat: A Dangerous, but Common Way of Entering Europe," Pew Research Center, April 30, 2014.

6 Nevine El-Aref, "The Man Behind the Leaks," *Ahram Weekly*, January 15, 2014.

7 In an interview with *Der Spiegel*, Sisi himself drew this comparison to justify the military takeover in Egypt. See Dieter Bednarz and Klaus Brinkbäumer, "Interview with Egyptian President Sisi: 'Extremists Offend the Image of God,'" Spiegel Online, February 9, 2015.

8 Passant Darwish, "Egypt's 'War on Atheism,'" Ahram Online, January 14, 2015.

9 Jack Shenker, "Sharm el-Sheikh Rumbles with Grand Promises of the International Elite," *Guardian*, March 15, 2015.

10 See https://www.youtube.com/watch?v=9Q6GaTOmWG4.

11 Alaa el-Sherbini, "Four Proposals and Three Job Offers from Sisi's Selfie," *Nogoum Misreyya*, March 17, 2015: http://www.nmisr.com/arab-news/egypt-news/99563 (Arabic).

EPILOGUE

1 Patrick Kingsley, "I'm No Traitor, says Wael Ghonim as Regime Targets Secular Activists," *Guardian*, January 9, 2014.

2 "Cameron Wins Airstrike Vote by Majority of 174—As It Happened," *Guardian*, December 3, 2015.

3 Ahmed Waguih, "Population Growth in Egypt."

RACHEL ASPDEN became literary editor of the *New Statesman* in 2006, at the age of twenty-six. She is now on staff at *The Guardian* and writes freelance for the *New Statesman*, *Observer*, *Prospect*, and *Think* magazine (Qatar). She lived in Cairo, Egypt, from 2003 to 2004 and worked as an editor and reporter for the English-language *Cairo Times*. In 2010 she was awarded a yearlong travel fellowship by the Winston Churchill Memorial Trust to research activists working to fight extremism within Islam. She is currently based in London.